the life and humor

of

Robin
Williams

the life and humor of

Robin Williams

jay david

A BIOGRAPHY

Quill

William Morrow

New York

It is the policy of William Morrow and Company, Inc., and its imprints
and affiliates, recognizing the importance of preserving what has been
written, to print the books we publish on acid-free paper,
and we exert our best efforts to that end.

Library of Congress Cataloging-in-Publication Data
David, Jay.
The life and humor of Robin Williams :
a biography / Jay David.—
1st ed.
p.   cm.
ISBN 0-688-15245-7
1. Williams, Robin, 1952 July 21—   2. Comedians—United States
Biography.   3. Actors—United States Biography.   I. Title.
PN2287.W473D38   1999
791.43'028'092—dc21
[B]   99-15806
CIP

Printed in the United States of America

FIRST EDITION

1   2   3   4   5   6   7   8   9   10

BOOK DESIGN BY NICOLA FERGUSON

www.williammorrow.com

Contents

The Improvisor

In spite of his love for an occasional raunchy, off-color routine, and in spite of the fact that most comedians seem to come from the wrong side of the tracks, Robin Williams was born to affluence and gentility. He had no bruising struggle to better himself economically; he faced no arduous climb up the ladder to fame and fortune. He was born the quintessential WASP—white, Anglo-Saxon, and Protestant from the get-go.

How this offbeat, contradictory man became one of the great twentieth-century improvisationists is a story that breaks all the molds and challenges all the clichés about the typical performer's blood, sweat, and tears.

Robin Williams was born in Chicago on July 21, 1952. He was a late arrival for his mother and father, who had each been married before; this was the second marriage for both of them. Almost fifty years old at the time of his son's birth, Robert Williams played from the beginning a rather remote role in the young boy's life.

Robin had two half brothers, but they were grown and had left home by the time of his arrival, so he was virtually an only child—the only child in the house, at any rate. The half brother on his father's side was named Todd Williams; the half brother on his mother's side was named McLaurin Smith, or sometimes Smith-Williams.

His father was vice president and midwestern regional manager of the Lincoln-Mercury Division of the Ford Motor Company—an imposing figure, and one to be treated with the utmost respect by any small-fry in the thirty-room house where the Williamses lived. That was a hard and fast rule: Robin addressed his father as "sir" most of the time. Later on, he would describe his father as "a very elegant man, like Lord Stokesbury, the viceroy of India."

Robin's mother was quite a different kind of person. A southerner, she was bubbling over with laughter, was full of fun, and led a very casual, almost totally carefree life. Laurie Williams has said that she and her son Robin were always close. As she put it: "His dad was a disciplinarian; I was the pal."

Funny though she was, she was not the only one who started Robin on his way toward being a comedian. Actually, she quoted him once as complaining that he had to leave home to get an honest laugh. Evidently, she was not completely attuned to his wacky humor. But she knew he was a very funny person.

For his part, Robin understood her humor and laughed at it, frequently calling her a "crazy southern belle." She spent some time with him; but when she was on her own, she socialized with her friends. In the evenings she went out to other peoples' homes and to parties. There weren't many hours that she spent with Robin.

When she was with him, though, "she was always funny," he recalled. "She had the jokes and the poems." Besides that, she played jokes on people.

She herself reminisced about an invitational dance she attended once at the Lake Forest—Lake Bluff (Illinois) Bath and Tennis Club. She wore a very stylish dress, every fold and crease in place, but she had obscured her two front teeth with Black Jack chewing gum, in the manner of a vaudeville comic. She remembered: "All the women were saying, 'You'd think someone who could afford clothes like that could afford to get her teeth fixed.' "

Her motto in life was "Man was put on Earth to know great joy." And she was determined to support that idea in everything she did.

But, to repeat, she was not always around. Robin grew up lonely. Here he was, plopped down in a thirty-room house with a nanny to care for him, trying to be a little boy—but with no other children anywhere in sight: "I was living on this huge estate. It was *miles* to the next kid."

What he did was agitate for toys, and the toys soon came.

He had at least two thousand soldiers and a battlefield in the basement where he could stage wars and make one army overcome the other. This battlefield had been the brainstorm of his father, who built a huge sandbox elevated on stilts above the basement floor. The family called it the "game table," and it became a place where Robin would spend hours sending fully rigged armies against one another in do-or-die scenarios that were always developing in the back of his mind.

This was the place where he started inventing not only armies but individuals. The best way to create individuals, he discovered, was vocally. He loved watching television, because on TV he could find many different kinds of people to use in his battle scenes. Jonathan Winters was a favorite of his; the man was funny, and a good mimic.

Once Robin got into the swing of voicing dramatic attacks on his battlefield, he began drawing from other television shows—from comedians as well as serious actors. "My imagination was my friend, my companion," he said once to a reporter for *Time* magazine.

Performing his battle scenes taught him to switch easily from one voice to another. One minute he'd be the Blue general running up a hill to challenge the Red general; the next minute, he'd be a soldier dying in agony, impaled on a fence. Then he'd be a cavalryman trying to disentangle himself from his downed horse.

At times the dialogue would overlap. Robin got very good at timing his vocal exchanges.

"I performed for my parents as a way of saying, 'Love me,' " he recalled later. "Waging those full battles tested my imagination, taught me the power of fantasy."

He also learned the value of being able to mimic other people, to be an endless number of individuals, and to change in a fraction of a second from one individual to another. In this way he could hold complicated conversations, with himself as an unlimited number of participants. It was here that he worked out the word-association routine that later became an important part of his improvisations.

Life was not dull in the Williams household. In fact, the family loved to move from one house to another in various communities around Detroit. At one time, Robin attended six different schools in eight years. This peripatetic existence did not seem to bother him. After all, he had his soldiers, and he had his numerous voices.

His school days, however, did not always sparkle. He was a bright boy, but he did not seem able to get along with others particularly well. In effect, he was spoiled, used to getting his own way most of the time. He was overweight and soft, and as a result of his lonely life, he wasn't used to scrapping for anything he wanted.

"I was fat and used to get beaten up a lot," he said. "They called me 'dwarf' and 'leprechaun.' "

He was always the "new boy," never staying long enough at one school to be really familiar. And like other alienated kids, he was always the target of jibes and catcalls in the schoolyard.

Robin's father may have been remote, but he was a solid man, perceptive about what was going on around him and with an unshakable sense of right and wrong. Robin grew up realizing that he had inherited an important depth of soul. About his father, he said: "He was a wonderful, ethical man who really thought . . . in terms of social issues, and about having a clear conscience about what you did."

As Robin reconstructed it all later on, his father must have finally become sick and tired of working in the automobile industry. "He really loved it when he started doing it, and when it became kind of *not*—the cars weren't good, and they were not selling them, and they were not making quality any more—he said, 'That's it. I don't want to do this anymore.' "

At first his father had been definitely enthusiastic about the Lincoln. "He was selling cars at a time when the Lincoln Continental was a real prestige car. But then things started going badly between labor and management, and he told me all these stories about the assembly-line workers sealing dead rats in the car doors because they weren't too happy with the situation."

Eventually, he lost all sense of pride in the workmanship of the company. "I'd see him come home looking almost pistol-whipped from being out there and hustling," Robin said.

This happened in 1969. Soon after that, the Williamses were on their way west. Robin was in high school, doing the best he could. Because of his father's position and his family's money, he was not in a public school; he was in an all-boys prep school in Birmingham, Michigan, where he had to wear a uniform: a tie and a distinctive blazer. He was not at all concerned about the change in venue, although—having led such a sheltered life—he'd never really seen much of the outside world except on television.

The Williamses now found themselves in another affluent community, but this one was light-years away in spirit from the Detroit suburbs they were used to. Tiburon was in Marin County, an enclave of the famous and well-to-do just north of San Francisco, past the Golden Gate Bridge. And there Robin Williams found an entirely new world.

"Suddenly I was at a gestalt high school," he told a reporter, "where students graduated if the energy was right."

It was a revelation. The school he transferred to was called Redwood High School, which more or less suggests the casualness of the area. This was a world diametrically opposed to the private schools he had been brought up in. Marin County had been deeply influenced by the counterculture of the 1960s, and it had a relaxed attitude that Robin had never seen before.

"Everyone was on acid." Yes, it was a crazy time, and the Bay Area was like a human game reserve. "Living there has made me what I am," he said.

Robin got into the action. He put himself on a stringent diet and lost the thirty or so pounds that had been making him look flabby and soft. Then he took up cross-country running, wrestling, and tennis. He suddenly blossomed into a different kind of person—outgoing, humorous, easy to talk to.

He also realized that he had a sense of humor, which no one had ever told him about before, and he began to use it to make friends among his classmates. By the time he graduated from high school he was named "Most Humorous" in the yearbook. He was also listed in a column titled "Least Likely to Succeed," but who cared about that.

Robin Williams was a changed man now, or at least a changed teenager. There were plenty of colleges he could go to, and plenty of subjects he could major in. Talking it over with his father, he decided on political science. He had always thought that his father would have been a good man in the United States foreign service, so why not Robin as well.

As for where he would go to school, he opted for what was then called Claremont Men's College in Claremont, California, not far from Los Angeles. He went to his classes dutifully, but he soon discovered that he had become distracted from political science and attracted by the theater.

Now all those hours of watching television comedies and dramas had their effect. When Robin was able to fill up his schedule with some courses other than political science, he decided to enroll in a theater class that was based on improvisation. He had always been able to make toy soldiers do things and say things. Couldn't he make people do things and say things, for college credit?

"It didn't just happen," he once explained. "It seemed to come naturally once I found it, but I created it through experimentation and playing with different things as a kid. I did it covertly—a closet comedian—until college, when I started to let it out in public."

It was the improvisation class that opened this door for him.

"I'd go to improv class and have a blast, and I realized, 'This really is exactly right. This is what I should do.' So I kept up with it." He perfected his skill and honed it to a sharp edge, until it was all Robin Williams and only Robin Williams.

He loved the course. All he had to do was get up and begin to make up scenes and talk them out in front of his fellow students. And he was funny enough now to get laughs whenever he wanted. He knew instantly that his interests lay here, in improvisation, and not in the foreign service.

"It was just a blast! I had so much fun that I failed all my other classes."

What happened at Claremont became known to his family in Tiburon at the end of the year. Robin flunked out. He discussed the situation with his father, who, to Robin's surprise, did not seem overly agitated about his interest in drama. He was quite supportive, in fact, and suggested that Robin change schools to study drama.

"If you love this," he told Robin, "do it. But have a backup profession, like welding."

According to Robin, he did visit a welding school to see what it was like. "I went to one welding class and the guy said, 'Before I begin, I'd like you all to know that you can be blinded by certain oxyacetylene torches.' " Robin said, "Excuse me. Thank you." And that was that.

Nevertheless, Robin was elated that his father supported his venture into acting. "I think somewhere in his life, *he* had a dream," Robin observed. "I don't know what it was, because he never really told me, but he had to give it up and come back home and support his family."

David Frost once asked Robin: "Going right back to the beginning, was there ever any evidence in the first few years, Robin, that you were going to end up doing what you were going to do? Because all the people we talked to said you were quite quiet."

Robin replied, "I think it was all kind of building up. . . . Better late than never—just kind of building up to the point where I finally left home."

Where to study drama, now that his father concurred with him that it might be a possible profession? This question was answered rather quickly when Robin enrolled at Marin College in Kentfield, California. The subject he concentrated on there was Shakespeare. He stayed for a year.

Marin College introduced him to Shakespeare, and he later found this helpful in filling out spaces in his rapid-fire standup improvisations. For example, here is a typical bit in which Robin becomes the playwright's agent:

"Will, we love you; seriously, we gotta lose the ghost, though. Will, this whole play's too Jewish. The whole Mom thing: What are you saying, what are you saying? Love it. You've got a black man here; the concept of a white family with a black child we'll buy, but a black man married to a red-haired white woman? Come on, Will! That's about two hundred years off. The interracial thing, Will, the queen's really worried. Not that she has her own hair, but we'll talk about that later."

During his year at Marin College, Robin learned to stretch himself dramatically more than ever before. Still, although he felt that Marin College might be all right for a beginning, he did not consider it the be-all and end-all of dramatic art. So he tried out for one of the stellar institutions in theater—the Juilliard School of Drama in New York City.

He was accepted. Having won a full scholarship to Juilliard—four years, from freshman through senior—he left the West Coast for New York City. At Juilliard, he would be studying under the noted actor and director John Houseman.

John Houseman had been associated with the New York theater for years and had been instrumental in helping Orson Welles found the Mercury Theater. Houseman would later become a huge success in the television series *The Paper Chase*, in which he played Professor Charles

W. Kingsfield, Jr., the nemesis of all Harvard Law students in contract law. He also was the voice in the classic commercials for Smith Barney, an investment company.

Robin Williams was instantly struck by Houseman's theatrical presence and decided that here was perhaps the best role model an aspiring actor could have. He buckled down to his class work with a vengeance.

Houseman realized that Robin was a special kind of person but did not at first see how to mold him into an actor. It was Houseman's sense of perfection that failed him here. Nor did any of his teaching associates know how to deal with this very special student.

Christopher Reeve, who became the star of the movie *Superman* and was later paralyzed in a fall from a horse, was a classmate of Robin Williams's. The two of them hit it off immediately. When Reeve was hurt, Robin was one of the first to visit him in the hospital and to bolster his spirits.

Reeve once said: "He wasn't your standard Juilliard product. Robin simply defied description"—and that was putting it mildly.

What the Juilliard faculty couldn't quite see was at the same time quite apparent to the students who were with Robin on a day-to-day basis. By his college years he had managed to perfect his machine-gun wit to a degree that no one could equal or even imitate. Every moment with his peers—would-be comedians—in the hallways of Juilliard, it was zap zap zap.

There were other attractions at Juilliard for Robin Williams. "I'd see these ballerinas and think they were goddesses," he said. "You'd see these women and you'd think they were formed like the most beautiful porcelain and you'd go, 'Excuse me, I'm only an actor, and I'm studying at Juilliard, but I think you're a goddess,' and they'd go [change to a lowlife, gum-chewing, bra-snapping broad]: 'Yeah. Well, get outta my face!' "

New York was the same mecca for all comedians then that it is today. In his hours off from the routine of class work at Juilliard—especially on weekends—Robin teamed up with another student and performed mime in whiteface in front of the Metropolitan Museum of Art, sometimes earning $150 a day. No words, just action. This miming was directly derived from the British buskers who performed in and around Covent Garden in London.

But mucking around in whiteface and making exaggerated gestures deprived Robin of what he knew was his greatest asset—his voice. After performing outside the museum lost its charm, he joined other students at the comedy clubs around New York City. There were good laughs to be had there. The money was a pittance, but Robin was not starving and, really, never would be.

While his high energy was driving his professors half crazy, he was gaining some control over it—something he had never been able to do before—and his comedy act was getting a little funnier. The newly harnessed energy was going in a specific direction, where Robin wanted it to go.

Christopher Reeve and Robin wound up together in the advanced class during Robin's third year. Reeve said, "They asked him to go back to the first-year level and start over again, I think simply because they didn't know what to make of him."

How this suggestion affected Robin Williams wasn't apparent; he was tight-lipped about it. In any case, though, he did not take the advice. Instead, as the story goes, he suddenly fell in love with a young woman, in typical collegiate fashion, and pursued her when she went to San Francisco.

Whether it was Juilliard's decision to demote him or whether it was his infatuation with this mystery girl, he never did return for his fourth year at Juilliard.

Instead, he settled down in San Francisco, only to find— again, as the story goes—that the love affair had been either one-sided or never really alive at all. To distract himself from his lost love, he took to visiting the comedy clubs around town, performing as he had done in New York.

He even tried out for theatrical roles in San Francisco, but openings were few and far between, and he didn't seem to have any luck in getting parts. This led him to concentrate more on the standup comedy clubs and coffeehouses that dotted the San Francisco Bay Area— clubs like the Boardinghouse and Holy City Zoo.

He was digging himself out of a deep hole, but he was not making himself any better for the future. Standup was a shield that he used to keep other people out of his face.

"I call character comedy my duck-and-cover technique for eluding commitments of any kind," he said once. "For a long time, it was just this ego fix of [needing] to get out there and get some laughs, because it's a great way of avoiding dealing with anything."

He put on a wry comic face and became clever little Robin: "They think I'm great. What's wrong with you?"

Since he wasn't getting any roles at all, he joined a comedy workshop in San Francisco and began to perform in some very small nightclubs throughout the Bay Area. One of his routines—parodying the Lawrence Welk show—earned him ten dollars when he performed it in a church basement.

He got a job as a bartender at an organic ice cream parlor, out in the boondocks. It was there that he met Valerie Velardi, a graduate student who was working as a cocktail waitress. She was really a modern dancer, she told him, but had to get some kind of work to tide her over the tight spots.

"When we met," Valerie recalled, "Robin was tending bar in a small club in San Francisco that featured comedians. I was so fascinated watching him behind the bar—his face going through a trillion changes in a matter of minutes—that I quit watching the comedians onstage. I became blatant about making eye contact with him—I definitely wasn't being maternal—and he reciprocated."

Robin remembered that night well. "I saw this beautiful, crazy Italian woman and started trying to catch her attention by acting crazy. A couple of nights later she saw me onstage in the same place and I could hear her saying to herself, 'This boy's not altogether well.' "

They began going out together. It was a short, intense courtship. "A month after our first meeting we began to live together," Valerie noted. "At that time I told him, 'You're the man who's going to marry me and give me my children.' He just didn't take it seriously."

"I just humored her for a while," Robin admitted.

They spent their first Christmas together on a skiing trip to Colorado with friends. Valerie would have been happier if she were with Robin alone, she later said. She was very interested in him; she sensed intuitively that he was an above-average comedian, but she also felt that he needed some kind of guidance. When he performed some of his routines for her, she realized that he was keeping all this crazy stuff in his head. She made a written catalog for him, organizing his routines into sections according to subject, and filed it away.

She also encouraged him with his comedy appearances. The money wasn't coming in the way it should be, and finally, in the summer of 1976, she persuaded him to try his luck in Los Angeles, where he might get that big break: a movie, or a shot on television.

He started out in L.A. at the Comedy Store on "open mike night," when any comedian who wanted to could appear. He later described it for *TV Guide* as "a terrorizing combination of the Roman arena and the *Gong Show*."

"My stomach was in my shoes, I was so scared," Robin recalled. "But after less than a minute I felt comfortable. I knew I could make people laugh." And he was right. Quite soon, he became a regular performer at the Comedy Store.

About a year later, in 1977, a producer named George Schlatter dropped into the Comedy Store looking for new talent. Schlatter had made television history by producing the original *Rowan and Martin's Laugh-In* in the late 1960s. The show had gone on for five years and had introduced Goldie Hawn to the world, along with Ruth Buzzi, Lily Tomlin, and dozens of other performers.

Now Schlatter wanted to produce a new show along the same lines. When he saw Robin Williams perform, he decided that he could use Williams's talent—if the comedian agreed to make certain changes:

[1] Cut off your shoulder-length hair.

[2] Shave off your beard.

Robin agreed. Schlatter liked his "fragmented free-associated act," and it went into the show. Unfortunately, though, the resurrected *Laugh-In* did not do very well on the air.

"The second *Laugh-In* was a good experience," Robin said. "It was like one of those things where everyone came on that show thinking, 'This is it! I'm going to be a big star,' and left going—gasp—'I'd better find other work.' "

On the strength of his work there, Robin did get a shot at another program, the *Richard Pryor Show*; but that, too, was short-lived—it folded almost immediately. Then he worked on *America 2-Night*, a "surreal talk show," with Martin Mull—which went belly-up after a very brief life.

Meanwhile, in June 1978, Valerie Velardi and Robin Williams had gotten married, and they needed money to start out as a family.

Space Alien

Robin Williams was ready for the big break that would make him a top-notch comedian. The only trouble was that the world was not yet ready for Robin Williams.

But then, in the somewhat mad but exciting way of show business, everything opened up for him and he was, quite abruptly, in.

The details of this breakthrough are interesting, since they bear no resemblance to the way things are supposed to go for someone on the way up.

Robin Williams's breakthrough depended on a number of completely disparate factors:

- ▲ A nine-year-old boy
- ▲ A hit film
- ▲ A hit television series
- ▲ An actor-turned-director

These apparently unrelated elements were strung together in a perfect concatenation—a unique scenario for success.

First let's take the hit television series, *Happy Days*. It had begun in January 1974, in the off-season just after the Christmas holidays. Ron Howard (noted for his longtime starring role with Andy Griffith in *The Andy Griffith Show* during the 1960s) and Anson Williams played high school buddies in a nostalgic take on the life of teenagers during the 1950s.

Happy Days was so popular that it had numerous spin-offs. The most notable in the mid-1970s was *Laverne and Shirley*, in which Laverne was played by the producer's sister, Penny Marshall. This spin-off lasted for four years, and *Happy Days* made it all the way through 1984.

Larry Brezner was an associate of Rollins, Joffe, Morra, and Brezner, an agency that represented entertainers. Brezner was constantly searching for new talent. One night he visited an improvisational comedy class in which Robin Williams was performing. Along with Robin was John Ritter, of the cast of *Three's Company*, another hit sitcom.

Brezner couldn't help noticing Williams: "I saw energy coming out of this person onstage that was shocking. Afterward, as soon as I could get him to slow down enough, we talked for five minutes. He told me he did standup, and I began following him around."

Meanwhile, the motion picture business—always in competition with television—was going through a revolutionary change. In 1977, *Star Wars*, one of the most popular films in decades, premiered and took the country by storm.

Star Wars, the brainchild of George Lucas, was heavily and masterfully promoted from its inception. Even before it opened, kids were clamoring to see it, and adults as well began taking an interest in this phenomenon. When it did open, it was greeted with cheers and settled in for a blockbuster run throughout 1977. The next year, it won seven Oscars for technical achievement. (One award was for John Williams's rousing militaristic score.)

One of those fascinated by the promotion of *Star Wars* and by the film itself was Scott Marshall, the nine-year-old son of Garry Marshall, the producer of *Happy Days*. Scott was so taken with the film that he had an important discussion with his father about the making of television shows. It was Scott who suggested that his father should have an alien—like those in *Star Wars*—visit the people in *Happy Days*.

Garry Marshall was not one to dismiss an idea simply because it came from a child, and he decided to have his writers work up an "alien visitation" episode. After a couple of tries, a suitable script emerged, and Marshall began casting it. The casting director for the episode was Jerry Paris, a longtime resident of the Hollywood comedy jungle. Paris had appeared as an actor in one of the comic hits of the 1960s, *The Dick Van Dyke Show*, so he knew comedy from the inside out.

Robin Williams appeared at the open audition held at the studio—just one of twenty actors intrigued by the idea behind the call. He was dressed as usual: rainbow suspenders, slacks, and a T-shirt. He was his usual rather silent, tightly wrapped self. He had been to dozens of these things; sometimes they paid off, and sometimes they didn't. He had no idea what this one might hold for him.

His turn finally came. Paris waved him on. There was conversation. Most of what was said between Paris and Williams was forgettable, except for one thing. It was Paris who explained the idea of an alien visiting *Happy Days*. "Now," Paris went on, "can you give me some idea of how you'd sit down as an extraterrestrial, for example?"

Robin said nothing. He went over to the couch and immediately sat on his head. The rest of the actors laughed instantly. So did Paris.

There was more. But that was what clinched the part for Robin—the immediacy of his action and the flair with which he did it. But of course it was only a role in one episode he was trying out for—hardly anything to write home about.

The "alien" episode was certainly different from the ordinary *Happy Days* routine. In it, Robin appeared as an alien from outer space sent to Earth to kidnap Ritchie Cunningham (the character played by Ron Howard). It was done in the style of *Happy Days*, though: light and wispy, with laughs interspersed here and there.

Robin played his role as the alien in a rather loose, goofy style, drifting onto the scene and appearing surprised and awed at the way earthlings acted; and he had invented words in a language that none of the earthlings understood.

He was able to work out a lot of the details at rehearsal, where the director and producer were more than pleased with the results. Then he went back to his Comedy Store routines to hone his style.

The alien episode eventually aired in February—and all hell broke loose. Seismographs could have recorded the shock waves. Mail poured in. The fans of the show loved Robin Williams as the alien—the letters begged for more. ABC-TV's executives didn't need much more than that to put together a scenario for the following season, September 1978. They didn't even bother with a pilot. Three men—Garry Marshall, Dale McRaven, and Joe Glauberg—sat down and plotted out a television series to play around the character that Robin Williams had already created, Mork from Ork.

An earlier show very, very similar to what they were trying to come up with here—called *My Favorite Martian*—had been a gentle spoof on what an alien would do on Earth. Ray Walston had played that alien, in the early 1960s, sprouting antennae at will, clothing himself backward, feeding his plants sandwiches and other delicacies while the dialogue spun on.

My Favorite Martian had been thin, almost one-dimensional. It was obvious that Robin Williams could give his character three solid dimensions, with his ability to utilize his whole body in putting over every line of dialogue. *Martian* had been limited to two starring roles, the alien and an earthling, played by Bill Bixby. The first difference, then, would be having a *woman*, not a man, play against the alien.

Marshall was gung ho about the new show, and he gave Robin Williams a great deal more leeway than he would have given another actor. For example, Robin was granted the unusual right to work over the scripts—that is, he did not have to say his lines exactly as they were written. He could improvise, which was his wont anyway. A great deal of the work could be done during rehearsals, with the writers supplying only a bare-bones outline of what Mork would be doing and saying in the framework of the basic story line.

The show became *Mork and Mindy*, with Pam Dawber as the female foil for Robin Williams's Mork from Ork. It was her job to keep the show on a realistic level so that all the capering and goofiness that characterized Robin Williams's role would not impair the essential believability of the story.

The character played by Robin was named Mork partly because he came from the planet Ork. In the series, Mork is exiled from Ork because his behavior has displeased his masters and associates. Unfortunately, he has a sense of humor, and he says what he believes, rather than what he should say. He has been overheard calling the biggest man on Ork "Cosmic Breath" rather than "Orson," which is his name.

For this he is sent to Earth to study the human race. The Orkans believe that, with his oddball sense of humor, he might be able to understand humanity better than they can. Earth has always been a mystery to Orkans, who have been around the planet but have never been able to fit in at all well.

Mork lands in a giant eggshell near Boulder, Colorado, in the Rockies. There he meets Mindy Beth McConnell, who is working as a clerk in a music store run by her father, Frederick. Mork is frank with Mindy; he tells her the truth about being exiled from Ork. She is puzzled by his strange clothing (he wears a suit but has put it on backward) and posture (he sits in a chair upside down). She agrees to let him stay in the attic of her apartment house and promises to help him adjust to Earth's strange ways as he studies the planet for his bosses back on Ork.

This was the background against which each episode of the show would play.

Robin brought much more to his role than a few facial quirks or comic gestures. In the first place, he was able to invent language—it used to be called double-talk in the 1930s—at will, and he did so. "Na-nu, na-nu. Hello, hello," became a byword throughout the country. And he would frequently go off into a long paragraph of "Orkan" gobbledygook for the amusement of the viewers.

In the second place, his facial tics added a great deal to the role. His rubbery features could stretch to almost any degree. His weird expressions, sometimes just the opposite of what a situation called for, were all part of the wild humor that emanated from him—enchanting the live audience in front of whom the sequences were filmed as well as the TV audience.

In the third place, he used his skill for vocal imitation to the nth degree. His trick of word association—which he had developed much earlier—was now perfected and completely under his control. He could zip from one person or situation to another in a split second. And he loved to talk to himself, back and forth, as he winged it.

But most of all, there was the general sense of wordplay at the core of his humor. He always relied on it, and he used it whenever it fit into a conversation—or the dialogue of the script. He had heightened his sense of wordplay for his Comedy Store routines, and that ability came in handy here.

In the long run, it was the artless and endearing manner Robin Williams evoked in his appearances before the camera that reached out and touched people. Slightly vulnerable always, with a genuine sweetness in his character, he played the role as if his rambling talk were absolutely unpredictable—as if he were talking not only to himself but to three or four parts of himself.

The sweetness and the appeal came through. The casting director at NBC once said: "You want to go up to him and pinch his cheeks." He had the innocence and enthusiasm of a child taking a first look at the world in all its glory.

During the taping of the first episode of *Mork and Mindy* there was an air of subdued excitement on the Paramount lot. It was obvious that all those letters were not the scheme of some press agent; they were the real McCoy. Howard Storm, the man assigned to direct most of the episodes of *Mork and Mindy*, remembered that first taping.

"Most of the time the studio audience for a new show is down. They don't know the characters. With Mork," he said, "they went crazy!"

Storm had little but good to say of Robin Williams and his talent. He called Williams a combination of Sid Caesar, Jonathan Winters, Marcel Marceau, and a little bit of early Danny Kaye. There was a kind of nonstop madness that appealed to Storm, no stranger to comedy, in Robin's work.

"Within the madness goes great discipline," Storm added. "I've never seen such freedom in a person who is basically shy."

"This guy is going to be a superstar with or without this series," said Dale McRaven, a cocreator of *Mork and Mindy*. "He's such an overwhelming personality that he could never play a regular sitcom husband with a wife and kids. It would be a waste of his talent, a waste of his craziness."

Robin Williams had his own thoughts about the madness that he was able to bring about with his routines. "It's madness all around. But the center is very calm, like the center of a hurricane."

True to his nature, Robin Williams was always on—

even between takes and between rehearsals. Whenever he was on the set, he was apt to break out into some kind of spontaneous routine. John Eskrow wrote of one that took place when he was covering the show for an article for *Rolling Stone*.

Just before the beginning of Monday's first read-through of the script, Robin leaped up, grabbed his crotch, and began stomping around the set, reciting in typical New York street growl:

"I gotcha, shazbot, right here, buddy. Yeah, here's your na-nu na-nu."

Jay Thomas, the actor playing Remo DaVinci, immediately returned the salute in kind, mockingly, and the two of them became street kids sparring on a corner. Thomas broke away, approached a full-length mirror, and kissed himself in the glass.

At that moment Tom Poston, who played a greeting card writer named Buckley and was dozing fitfully behind a pile of scripts, woke up just long enough to add an indistinguishable comment, probably lewd. Meanwhile Pam Dawber, playing Mindy, yawned and made for the telephone, where she was spending her morning battling boredom.

The director, Howard Storm, was pacing the floor, blocking out the first scene of the script—a delicatessen opening up in Boulder that the DaVincis had come to run. By then, Thomas and Robin had broken up their duel and were seated together. Storm turned into a Little Italy deli speaker: "Whatzit, jus' da two of yiz?"

Now Robin was crouching down, pawing at an imaginary door, wailing forlornly for food.

The Italian restaurateur became an old Jewish shopkeeper: "Go away from here, dis is a place of beeznis, you kids."

This kind of thing would go on day after day, until sometimes it tended to get out of hand. But Storm always kept it within bounds so that time was not wasted on too much horseplay.

Storm did like a happy set, and he managed to keep it that way—especially with the talents of Robin Williams always at his call.

The read-through began shortly after that, with Mork discovering a new aspect of human behavior unfamiliar to him. In this case it was the fact that the DaVincis were simply arguing about nothing at all. However, when brother and sister made up warmly after the argument, Mork decided that he would argue with Mindy in order to have a final reconciliation with her—since the DaVincis' had been so warm and so personal.

The script was larded with one-liners, but it suffered from first-draft-itis; and as the one-liners came up one after the other, spirits began to sag. Robin's lines were always better.

"Sorry, kids, we can't go to the zoo. Mindy ate all the endangered species."

But, of course, a kook is much easier to write for than a normal guy.

The reading stopped for some thoughts of Robin's on

Pam's reaction to the jokes. "Maybe she could make fun of my hair," Robin suggested, pretending to grab for her behind. This amused her and she started to giggle. Storm let the horseplay go on for a few more minutes and then rapped for attention, and the reading went on.

Robin Williams was in an unusual situation on *Mork and Mindy*, responsible not only for improvising his own lines but also for keeping the actors stimulated in the boring times between takes.

Later on Robin Williams hammed it up with a takeoff on "Mr. Rogers," the dim but lovable host of a kiddie show. "Welcome to my neighborhood. Let's put Mr. Hamster in the microwave oven. OK. Pop goes the weasel!"

Other characters leaped out of his mouth: Ernest Sincere, a used-car dealer of the lowest order. Joey Stalin, a Russian standup comedian. Little Sherman, a nasty young kid. The Beverly Hills Blues Singer, Benign Neglect, singing: "Woke up the other day. Ran out of Perrier. I've really paid my dues. Had to sell my Gucci shoes."

Then Robin became an old codger with a high-pitched, quavering voice—Grandpa Funk. He explained how he had once been a standup comedian with a TV series about an alien. "Of course that was before the real aliens landed." Pause. "Anyone in the audience remember World War III—all forty-five minutes of it?"

Within weeks, *Mork and Mindy* climbed heavenward in the Nielsen ratings, and it soon stood at the top of the weekly list. It firmed up usually in the top ten—basically a smash hit for a sitcom.

Instantly magazines and newspapers zeroed in on Robin Williams, giving the background on his rise to the top, along with anecdotes about his early life and his rise in comedy. And, of course, they asked him how he looked at that strange extraterrestrial brainchild he had perfected all on his own.

Robin said, "Mork is ever the optimist." Robin was trying to think through how this simple invention from his fertile mind had struck such a chord in the public imagination. "Everything is all right because he's an alien. He has a whole globe and society to look at for the first time. He's traveled all over the universe and talked to inanimate things. So it's not unusual for him to discuss matters with a moose head or his space suit. He's unsure if they are real and he doesn't want to risk offending anything."

Valerie Velardi, his wife, had ideas, too. "Mork is ingenious and childlike, and wonderful. Robin has a lot of that in him. He has three-hundred-and-sixty-degree vision, and he reacts sensitively to everything around him. When we first met, I noticed that his naive zaniness can lead people—especially women—to believe he needs mothering. I take care of that particular child at home, usually on Sundays after a week of twelve-hour days on *Mork and Mindy* when he's wiped out. I call him my autistic son at those times. He's Little Andrew who has to be asked to pick up his clothes."

Going along with his wife's analysis, Robin continued: "Some women feel protective toward me. I guess it's because Mork is very childlike. They think of him as naive, which allows me to get away with a lot of things. He's innocent and there's some of that in my own nature."

The freedom he demanded in his contract helped him from the beginning, he believed. "There's no pressure when I'm improvising, because I'm given the freedom to create. It's chancy, but I have a sense of relaxation, an inner calm, when the craziness is going on. I haven't dried up yet on camera, but some things don't work as well as I hope. I've been lucky."

Not surprisingly, because of its instant popularity and overwhelming success in the Nielsen ratings, *Mork and Mindy* became the talk of the industry. People even talked about Williams winning awards for his comic mastery. And he did win a Golden Globe Award in 1979 for his work on *Mork and Mindy* during the first year of production in 1978. Not only did he win a Golden Globe, but that same year he got a Grammy Award as well, for an album of his standup work titled *Reality . . . What a Concept!*

It was obvious that things were breaking just right for him.

The first year *Mork and Mindy* was on, it wound up third from the top of all shows on television, tied with its progenitor, *Happy Days*. But that distinction did not last long. In 1979, the network—ABC-TV—decided to begin playing the scheduling game with the show.

Mork and Mindy was moved from Thursday night to Sunday night. Nothing was wrong with Sunday, except that everyone had grown used to Thursday night as Mork night—and the show was now slotted opposite Archie Bunker, an extremely popular and long-lasting champion in the ratings wars.

The ABC-TV brass had made a fundamental error in not paying attention to the ancient saw: "If it ain't broke, don't fix it." By the end of its second year, the show plummeted from its spot in the top ten to the thirty-fourth ranking.

Now there were scurryings about and frantic phone calls and all kinds of skull sessions. In an interview in *TV Guide*, Pam Dawber said Robin Williams had decided that Mork should become a little more sophisticated. However, she did not blame him for what then happened:

"That was a big mistake. But I think Robin and I were both innocent bystanders. The ideal formula for *Mork and Mindy* is to make Mork the little buffoon who messes up the situation and then, out of naïveté, saves the day. Mork is a Chaplinesque character. He is simple.

"When Robin decided that Mork should be more sophisticated, the producers and writers went along with him. Robin was too close to the character to see it. They weren't. Then they added all those other crazy characters and the show lost all sense of reality and balance. It just stopped being funny."

One of those "other crazy characters" was Raquel

Welch, brought in to beef up the ratings. She lasted for two weeks. "The stress during those two weeks was almost unbearable," Pam Dawber noted.

Garry Marshall agreed with Dawber. "That's when we realized that we had fallen into the world of competition and greed. With the Raquel show we went down the sewer. From then on, he knew we wanted to get back to the original, simple concept."

In spite of all the patching up and fixing, the show did not really get back on track, even when it was switched from Sunday night back to Thursday night. One of the last desperate measures to save the show occurred in 1981, when Jonathan Winters was added to the cast as Mork's son, named Mearth (pronounced "mirth").

Garry Marshall said, "We were dead in the water at the end of last season. We cut our audience by tinkering, almost lost it completely when the network put us up against Archie Bunker on Sunday night. We decided to marry Mork and Mindy, and when the chance to involve Jon appeared, we snapped at it."

Actually, Winters was Robin Williams's idea, not Marshall's. Marshall commented, "Frankly, I think ABC was surprised when Robin made such a strong pitch in June—they expect stars to storm in, threatening to leave unless they get their salary tripled, with all the money in gold up front. And I think they were just as surprised when Jonathan agreed."

The marriage of Mork and Mindy did occur, and their

honeymoon took place on Ork, which proved to be full of strange unearthly creatures. According to the strict rules of Orkan life, Mork became pregnant and laid an egg from his navel; the egg grew and grew until it opened to reveal a full-grown Jonathan Winters.

But somehow the fun was gone. In spite of some hilarious, unforgettable scenes between Robin Williams and Jonathan Winters, the series was in a free fall.

While the show was in decline, though, the career of Robin Williams was definitely not. He had managed to garner an extremely wide range of fans in his television appearances. And exposure of any kind has never hurt an actor.

In spite of the oddball image he had attained as the alien from Ork, some of the episodes were classics. In fact, when *TV Guide*, in the summer of 1997, selected the one hundred greatest episodes of all time, one episode from *Mork and Mindy* was featured: "Mork's Mixed Emotions," which had aired on May 6, 1980.

Others in the business were just as cognizant of Robin's talent, and films were beckoning him. Nor was Robin one who could fail to heed those lovely beckonings. And so for a while he found himself working both in television on his series and in films as well.

"I Yam What I Yam"

Chapter Three

The main benefit Robin Williams derived from his four years of work on *Mork and Mindy* was a sensationally large amount of public exposure. This exposure had made his name a household word, of course, and in no way could he regret that. But he had not been challenged much as an actor.

As his television run as Mork went on, Williams began to feel a distinct lack of professional progress. In short, Mork the alien was a dead end. Mork was a result of Williams's talent as a standup comedian, not his genius for acting. What he needed, then, was something just a bit more demanding, dramatically.

Actually, the agency that represented him had been searching everywhere for a possible film. Robin had done one movie in 1977, an obscure film called *Can I Do It . . . Until I Need Glasses?* It had more or less vanished from sight—and so much the better, as far as Robin was concerned.

It was in 1980 that the agency found a

proper vehicle for Robin Williams's talent, a motion picture version of the comic strip *Popeye*. The character Popeye had appeared in movie houses in the 1930s and 1940s in a very popular series of short animated features whose theme song, "Popeye the Sailor Man," became familiar to movie fans and is still well known. But that was a cartoon Popeye. The new film would feature a live Popeye, played against a real background, though the story line would be similar to the comic strip created by E. C. Segar in 1929. Very simply, it was a quest story: Popeye in search of his long-lost father, "Poopdeck Pappy."

Casting Robin Williams was a crucial decision—and it was Williams himself who managed to assure the makers of the film that he was the one to play Popeye. The director and producer was Robert Altman, famous for many quirky, offbeat films. Altman had created a smash hit when he filmed *M*A*S*H* in 1970, a black-humor novel set during the Korean War that made a personal statement about war and valor. He had also done *McCabe and Mrs. Miller* (1971), with Warren Beatty and Julie Christie; and he had directed *Quintet*, a rather sour story about a deadly game of hide-and-seek in a frozen world of the future. Despite a somewhat uneven record, Altman was a proven talent of the film world, and Robin Williams knew he was lucky to be working with him. Yet Altman made abnormal demands on his actors. He ran a film shoot in his own inimitable style, working with his own special ideas; he was quite capable of exerting full control over everyone involved.

Popeye was not shot in the usual Hollywood studio or on location somewhere nearby. Instead, Altman leased a large piece of land on the island of Malta in the Mediterranean, and he spent four and a half months there with an international construction crew of 165 workers, designing and building a village he called "Sweethaven," where the action would take place.

The village had nineteen buildings—all of them complete four-sided structures, unlike the one-sided frontages of, say, a typical Western movie street. Altman and his crew produced an imaginary nostalgic town, set against rolling hills, with steeples and balconies rising against the skyline. The whole was threaded with wooden sidewalks in the style of ramshackle old New England towns during the era of the great whaling expeditions.

This background was exactly right for *Popeye*, a cartoon strip in which life took on a peculiar timelessness—today at one moment, and a thousand years ago at another. The caricatures in Segar's cartoon strip are deliberate exaggerations of human beings, of houses, of ships, of everything depicted. The dialogue is clipped, distorted, truncated. "Eeeek!" means "Help!" "Ugh!" means "I don't like it"—and so on.

Altman approached the film *Popeye* with some diffidence. He knew he had to keep a tight rein on things from beginning to end. "The biggest problem we had making *Popeye* is that we had no norm to fall back on," he said. Of course, *Superman* had been made into a film with living characters. But the exaggerations in that case were the things that men could and could not do. Superman could fly, with the help of special effects, and so could Batman. *Popeye*, however, was not sci-fi or derring-do: it was more like an old-fashioned romance.

"If I'm dealing with Texas or New York, I can say, 'Oh, this is the way it happens, you ride up on a horse, or you take a taxi,' " Altman said. "But with *Popeye*, we had to create everything. I like doing that. Most of the films I've made deal with aliens—people in a strange land who don't belong there and are trying to cope. I like to tell a story about an alien wandering into a strange place. It's easier to deal with, for one thing. A contained society is easier dramatically. I don't have to deal with the real world. I need an imagined world, set apart, and then an outsider coming into it."

Mainly, the problem of putting a character like Superman on film with real people is solved simply by dressing him up in the proper attire, even with a mask if necessary. But for the character Popeye, the problem was different. Altman had thought about it a great deal, and he knew he would have to compensate somehow in order to get the look he wanted: "I wanted a different look. I wanted a roundness, even though the characters are two-dimensional. I wanted a tone and sense of realism, but not in a literal way, I mean not compared to something."

Altman went on, "I muted the colors, the town. As the film progresses, the colors become more specific, cartoony. The reds come out. The wardrobe changes. And it's more crowded at the beginning; you have a sense of a lot of people and activity. It's sparer by the end."

There was no mask for Popeye to wear; there were no special clothes for Olive Oyl. What the audience saw was exactly what was there. Popeye had his face twisted against that corncob pipe all the time. He spoke around the pipe whenever he opened his mouth. His words were muddled; his speech was mushy.

When Robin Williams arrived on the island of Malta in the spring of 1980, he felt that he had been rescued from an imminent disaster. *Mork and Mindy* was in a slump after only one year of success, and no one seemed to know how to get it back on track. Besides that, Robin himself had gotten into a rut. He was spending most of his time on the set and then, at night, at the Comedy Store and other such places. And there were parties—endless parties.

"In Hollywood," Robin said, "they see me and say, 'Brilliant!' instead of 'Hello!' You lose perspective. It's salvation to get out of America and see myself from another point of view."

Robin and Altman had long discussions about the role of Popeye. Robin said that he had been thinking of how to do the part for a long time, ever since 1979, when he had first learned about the go-ahead from Altman. He told Altman he loved the idea of being Popeye: "When people think of cartoons, they think of Road Runner, but the objective of this movie is to make the characters, strange and bizarre as they are, into people, to give them souls."

Robin was asked how it felt to be working on his first movie—disregarding the low-cost potboiler he had appeared in earlier.

"Making your first movie, you wonder if you can make the transition from TV to the big screen," he confessed. "If you can act—take all that madness and confine it within a character. There's always doubt."

The script of *Popeye*, written by Jules Feiffer, the cartoonist and satirist, was an attempt to build up a biographical history of the people in the cartoon strip—Olive Oyl, Wimpy, and Popeye. The focus was, of course, on Popeye. In writing the script, Feiffer kept in mind Altman's main concerns: keeping the characters real but making them exaggerated and bigger than life.

Feiffer had his own take about what the creator of Popeye was saying in the cartoon strip: "Segar's essential vision," he said, "is that the world we're living in is without structure, is short of ideas, of leaders, of passion, of belief in almost everything; and although everything may be in a muddle throughout the community of Sweethaven, the Oyl family and Popeye will endure."

In Feiffer's script, Popeye arrives at Sweethaven in a blinding thunderstorm. From the start, as in a typical Western, everybody treats him as the mythical "stranger"—an interloper, an "enemy"—and does everything possible to push him out of town. Instead of the villain, such as a rich rancher, who runs a town in a Western, *Popeye* has an invisible dictator called "the Commodore," whose dirty work is done by the snarling brute Bluto.

All of the rooming houses turn Popeye down, except for Olive Oyl, whose life is already in disarray. She's engaged to Bluto, but agrees to board Popeye, and he moves in. He's searching for his lost father, he tells her. They begin to regale each other with their life stories, and soon enough discover Swee'Pea, the little "orphink," in a basket on Olive's doorstep.

Action. Bluto kidnaps Swee'Pea and Olive. Popeye has to search for them, and in the process he does in most of Bluto's henchmen and, finally, Bluto himself. It's all there in the colorful frames of the original cartoon strip.

Feiffer tried to get the dialogue as close as possible to the familiar cartoon-strip "balloon." As a result, some of the dialogue is difficult to understand, and in the case of Popeye, some of it doesn't quite get past the corncob pipe.

For Robin Williams, one important difference between *Popeye* and *Mork and Mindy* was that Altman did not allow him to do any improvisation with the script. He could improvise actions and gestures, but tampering with the dialogue was strictly verboten.

This was a change of pace for Williams, and it carried over into his behavior between takes. He did not create the zany, hilarious improvisations that the cast of the television series had enjoyed. Instead, he pretty much minded his own business and concentrated on how he appeared onscreen.

And it was Popeye's actual appearance that mattered most to Altman. He wanted that corncob pipe to be sticking out of Popeye's mouth at all times. He wanted that one-eyed stare, so characteristic of the cartoon frames. He wanted the slouch and the lurch of the animated Popeye in the cartoon shorts.

The absense of horseplay put Robin Williams on the alert. He worked hard to get Popeye's diction, as well as his looks, just right. Jules Feiffer's script, of course, played constantly on the well-known malapropisms that Popeye uttered in the daily cartoon strip. It also paid particular attention to his habit of muddling *k*'s and *t*'s so that "squint" became "squink" and "orphan" became "orphink."

Yet in spite of being reined in by the producer-director, Robin Williams managed to make himself persona grata to the cast. Paul Dooley, the actor who played Wimpy, the moocher, found the star a decent, friendly person. "It's a cornball word, but Robin's humility, his down-to-earth quality, is what gets everyone. You would expect this comedy star to be larger than life, but he's so laid back, so concerned with what's going on with other people, so giving as an actor, that it's been a revelation."

Robin's wife, Valerie, had been hired as an assistant,

keeping notes on various details that needed attention. She was always there for Robin after a hard day's work. She did what she could to keep him on an even keel throughout the filming, even when tensions developed.

On one occasion Robin and Valerie spent a four-day weekend in Paris, returning with a pair of baby shoes for the wife of Van Dyke Parks, the music arranger, who had given birth to a baby girl on Malta.

And Williams became the company joker after hours, helping boost morale. "His mind is so fast you can't believe it," Dooley remarked. Another actor, Robert Fortier, said: "Give him two bottle caps, and it's instant comedy."

During his off hours, Williams spent most of his time rehearsing singing and acrobatics, which were not his primary accomplishments. Or he might jog around the set in an old sweatshirt.

Actually, though, he did not have to build up his forearms; he was given an artificial pair made of rubber and plastic. They were clumsy, but with practice he learned to manipulate them without too much distress. Along with his squint—that is, his one-eyed stare—and the corncob pipe always stuck in his mouth, this was the image he presented to the audience. He was the living embodiment of the character in the comic strip.

Ray Walston, who had been the featured player on the television series *My Favorite Martian* from 1963 to 1966, was cast as Popeye's father. The fact that he had played a Martian had not helped Walston's career—

which changed for the better when he was cast as the irascible judge in *Picket Fences* in the 1990s. But about Robin's career, Walston was encouraging. "Robin's series won't bother him as mine did me," he said. "He's able to kid the pants off that thing and make a mark for himself as an excellent comedian. And he's a devoted actor. In the next years, whether as an actor, comedian, or screen personality, Robin Williams will go on to things the likes of which Hollywood has never seen!"

Altman himself, in a moment of insight, said this: "There are those who are great actors, and there are also those who are so creative that they add a rare dimension to whatever they do. If I hadn't had Robin, I wouldn't have made *Popeye*."

In a rare mood of seriousness, Robin Williams confided that his improvisational humor had a number of shortcomings.

"I have wonderful beginnings," he said. "I'd play with them, but most of the time I couldn't find endings, so I developed a style in which I pieced things together, going from one to another with no transition. Sometimes I'd go too far and lose people."

There were deeper levels to Robin Williams's personality than most onlookers thought. He was very frank with one magazine writer.

"When you're not being funny, sometimes things can be really tense. The world situation scares me so! My essential fear is that with all the weapons at the disposal of world leaders, they could end the world very easily, if not with nuclear weapons, then with poison gas or germ warfare. Somehow or other, a situation may come where someone could pull the cork. That fear makes me want to create as much as possible before that happens—also, maybe try to have some influence on stopping it if I can.''

Generally speaking, the critics tried to like *Popeye*, though they didn't really relish it. Pauline Kael's review said, in conclusion: ''You don't get much pleasure from it, but you can't quite dismiss it. It rattles in your memory. Would the film have come together better if it had been simpler—without so much 'environment'? Maybe—if Robin Williams had broken through, if he had felt free enough to make the role his own. But how could he feel free, all screwed up and using only one eye?''

Time wrote: ''Popeye, as played by Robin Williams, appears to be undergoing an identity crisis far beyond the powers of spinach cure. As a result his moral force—and he was once one of the great comic-strip exemplars of righteousness tied to a short fuse—appears sicklied o'er with the pale cast of self-absorption.''

David Ansen of *Newsweek* was also negative: ''Williams is wonderfully endearing and inventive (and perhaps responsible for some of the off-the-cuff wit). But one senses an explosive talent held on a tight leash.''

Vincent Canby of the *New York Times* put it this way: ''Playing the title role is Robin Williams *(Mork and*

Mindy), a terrifically funny actor, especially when he is free to work variations on his material, something that, obviously, he could not be allowed to do here. . . . Then, too, this *Popeye* is a musical, which is to say, a film-with-music, and there's not one member of the cast who can really sing."

Starring in *Popeye* was an unfortunate debut for Robin Williams. The reviews deplored his very hard efforts to play the role the way Altman had envisioned it—Altman's concept had proved to be more a problem than a solution.

Yes, Robin did look like Popeye, with the pipe clenched in his teeth, angled skyward, and his squinty eye usually clamped tight shut. But this pose itself was enough to destroy anything Robin could have done with his voice.

In fact, most of Robin's dialogue had to be lip-synched again after the film was in final cut. Even so, many of his words were simply burblings that seemed to erupt out of a deep well.

Along with the squint and the pipe, there were the plastic forearms used to reproduce the exaggerated muscles of the original comic strip. The many problems created by trying to act out a line drawing realistically were, in the end, too much for the film to bear.

Popeye was not a total failure, but it became a failure in Robin Williams's mind when the critics got going on him, and it put a crimp in his film career. In some circles, the word was already out that he was through; and no one seemed interested in signing him up for another screen role. For a while, he was still working on *Mork and Mindy*, but when that show was canceled by the network, he did what was typical for him: he went back to his standup comedy and tried to work out some new routines.

Garp According to Robin

In 1978, the author John Irving published his most popular book, *The World According to Garp*. He had already written several quirky seriocomic novels—*Setting Free the Bears* (1968), *The Water-Method Man* (1972), and *The 158-Pound Marriage* (1974). But *Garp* was to be his biggest and best book yet, and also his kookiest.

Briefly, the plot is as follows: Garp was conceived during World War II, when his mother, Jenny Fields, a New England heiress, gave herself to a brain-damaged airplane gunner who was able to shout only the meaningless word *Garp*!

Garp was born as T. S. (for Technical Sergeant) Garp and later became an author. His mother wrote a book titled *A Sexual Suspect*—a statement on feminist rights—and became a leader in the women's rights movement.

Garp fathered two children, Duncan and Walt, by his wife, Helen. In an automobile accident, Walt was killed, Duncan lost an eye, and Helen was severely injured. Garp went to live in a home for battered women where a cult called the Ellen Jamesians lived; Ellen was an eleven-year-old girl who had been raped.

Then Garp wrote a novel, *The World According to Bensenhaver*, dealing with ghastly happenings and other awful things; for Garp, life imitated art. Jenny was killed by a madman, and Garp himself was shot by a woman who thought he had raped her sister. He hadn't.

Numerous characters roamed about in Irving's novel; one of whom was the transsexual Roberta Muldoon, formerly Robert Muldoon, a tight end for the Philadelphia Eagles.

Robin Williams was fascinated by the Irving novel, which he read while shooting *Popeye*. He was particularly intrigued by the main character. Garp was essentially a loser, but underneath that reckless exterior he was thoroughly decent and put upon. The contradictions in the character fascinated Robin, and he carried the book around with him, referring to it again and again as something about Garp's relationship to life itself would strike him.

George Roy Hill had also developed an interest in Garp. Hill was the man who had made the hit movies *Butch Cassidy and the Sundance Kid*, *The Sting*, and *Slaughterhouse Five*. He was aware of the success of *Mork and Mindy*, of course, and he realized that Robin Williams might be just the man to tackle the role of Garp.

During Robin's third year on *Mork and Mindy*, a deal

was arranged with Hill, and the papers were signed for Robin to play the part of Garp in a movie version of the book. The movie was scheduled for shooting in the late summer of 1981.

But this was not a done deal for some time. There were problems from the very start. Hill admitted that he was not totally secure in casting Robin Williams as Garp.

"A lot of people thought I was crazy to cast Robin," he told *New York* magazine. "But you make these decisions instinctively. I'd seen him as Popeye and didn't understand a word he said. I'd seen him once as Mork and didn't understand him [then] either. I thought he was just a standup comic. But on meeting him, I felt he had a sense of decency that was important. Garp is an abrasive man, but his underlying decency is a key part of the character, and I felt Robin was the sort of actor who might provide that."

Later on, Hill expanded on his comments about Robin Williams: "Robin is an extraordinary talent," he said. "He's an actor, a real actor, not just a comedian who is put into a role requiring acting."

The main problem, as Hill analyzed it further on into his working relationship with Robin Williams, was Robin's delivery. "Robin had a habit we had to overcome. He's inclined to a too-fast delivery—it took me a long time to slow him down to a playing speed."

As for Robin himself, he loved the part. But he also saw problems. What troubled him most was that John Irving had written the book in such a way that each episode plays in a different time frame. It was up to Robin to try to keep these phases in sync. As he put it:

"The main problem is in making all the different ages fit together. I have to make all those phases of life and the different relationships believable. . . . Performing for an audience is more like gliding or flying. Playing Garp is a scraping-away process."

When he played Popeye for Robert Altman, the role had been a kind of impersonation—a corncob pipe, a squint, a shambling gait. Garp was very different.

"Popeye was just playing in a sense, just guts and bones, very grounded. My other stuff is more flighty and fancy. Playing Garp is really stretching to go down to the sinews and open up your muscles."

When shooting began, Robin refused to look over the rushes each night. He had been burned somewhat by the critics for his interpretation of Popeye, and playing Garp was very tricky and very demanding. It required instinct, professionalism, and experience. Frankly, Robin was a bit scared.

When the film was almost in the can, he explained why he had not wanted to see the rushes: "I'm afraid they would jar me. I don't think I'll get a view of myself until the final cut. It's like drowning, like running for your life. . . . I finished one day of shooting and thought, 'God, I died.' Even though it was only a single scene, I had this bizarre feeling and I wept for a couple of hours after it.

When I finally see the film, I'll look back and say, 'I did that.' I'll be proud. I feel proud now, but I just can't say it yet because it's not over. It's a gamble.''

As it happened, this was a time of no confidence for *Mork and Mindy*, too. There had been a big slump in the ratings in the show's second and third seasons, and this brought up more things for Robin to worry about.

"That was kind of depressing at first because I took it on myself personally, thinking, 'Oh, God! I'm not funny anymore.' At last I realized that it was a combination of other things. They were screwing around with the schedule, changing the time slot every other night.''

The unsettled situation on *Mork and Mindy* tended to depress Robin: "Sometimes I feel like I could be back to ground zero again. I go through these phases of getting terrified. I can't really cope with them because they're debilitating. I have to try new things—like *Garp*—to push myself out. You know—the next chance.''

Robin was somewhat surprised by the interest that the author of *Garp*, John Irving, showed in the making of the film. Irving would show up on the set now and then, offering advice and getting into discussions about Garp with Robin. He would sometimes underline certain passages from the book and give them to Robin.

"He would come up and say, 'Read this passage,' '' Robin recalled. "Especially in the last scene, the death scene, he underlined the whole passage of what Garp's whole attitude is while he's dying. And it's helped incredibly; the book was very specific. That's why at the end, hopefully, even though it is death or whatever, he still has a positive monument to his life. He's still, you know, 'I'm flying, I'm flying.' That's the whole thing about flying versus the undertoad.''

"Undertoad" was a word John Irving had coined to describe the forces of doom and mortality in the book and the film. The "undertoad" was worse than simple fate. It could erupt in acts of violence, cruelty, weakness, and sexual abuse.

Robin could see that Garp's life had been hell to live—and even to die—but in spite of all the hellishness around him, Garp lived heroically, and he wrote with comic wisdom and even compassion at the end.

That was what puzzled Robin. He was having trouble thinking through the acting he had to do to project the heroic vision underlying the theme of the "undertoad." In this regard, Robin got most of his advice from George Roy Hill, who was good at explaining the acting process.

"You're more a reactor to things than an actor," Hill told Robin. The idea was that he was more acted upon than an actor in action—to put it in rather awkward theatrical terms. Hill continued, "Listen, if you're going to do this, you're going to have to accept the fact that you have a presence and you're not to try and do something just because you're on film. Just know that when you're on camera, you don't have to worry. If you're thinking thoughts, the camera will register them.''

"He put me at ease on that point," Robin noted. Thinking about his role as Garp, he continued, "I knew it was in there. I just had to dig it up, tap into those things I'd kind of put away during the last four years of doing television."

And that led him to the following:

"There's a side that—like Garp—is very sensitive, painfully aware of things, painfully aware of injustice and pain. It's a sensitivity. Sometimes I'm bordering on hyper-sensitivity. I can cover it up by making fun of it and laughing about it. I can chuck it off, but deep inside I'm going, 'Oh God!'

"It scares me sometimes, the state of things in the world right now. . . . My ultimate fear is the annihilation of nuclear war. I mean, that's the real undertoad."

And that is what Robin Williams eventually managed to put into the role.

The man who wrote the screenplay for *Garp*—Steve Tesich—was very much in accord with the kind of acting Robin was doing. "He's the only person who could do this role," Tesich said. "There's an openness to him, an accessibility that you just don't find in actors anymore. He can do the hardest thing of all—portray a human being and not an exaggerated caricature of a human being."

Other members of the cast felt much as Tesich did. John Lithgow, who played Garp's brawny transsexual buddy Roberta, said that he had racked his brains for months, trying to think who could play Garp: "When they announced Robin Williams, I thought, 'What a fantastic idea.' Like Garp, he has a kind of earnestness about him, an off-the-wall sense of humor and an underlying sense of sadness. I can't think of any actor who might duplicate that."

Glenn Close, a freethinking woman, a strong feminist, and a leader in the women's movement, played Garp's mother, Jenny Fields. Close was particularly surprised and pleased by the compassion that Hill brought out in Williams's acting: "Robin's one of the smartest people I've ever met, and it was amazing to watch him and George work out. Robin brings out that wonderful warmth of Garp. Someone described Garp as a mother man, or man mother, and I think it's a great description."

In his first look at Garp, Robin Williams had deliberately disregarded the obvious similarities between this character and Mork; and in fact the two characters are very dissimilar in terms of environment and milieu.

"It would be like saying, 'Compare and contrast Mickey Mouse and Moby-Dick,'" Robin told a reporter at one point.

There would be no "Garp and Mindy" then?

Robin went into one of his standup improv routines. First he was an officious, snide announcer: "*Garp and Mindy*—a new series on ABC!" Then he was the interviewer: "Mr. Williams, will you be going back to TV?"

"No!"

A split second later he was a TV executive, with a smarmy smile: "A million dollars."

Robin: *"Garp and Mindy*, you got it. Where do I sign? Okay!"

Robin had always had fun with his press interviews. He would instinctively indulge in mocking improvisations. A simple answer might turn into a small theater of improv—half a dozen different characters, voices, and scenes.

For an interviewer from the *Washington Post*, Robin recalled one of the first nights when *Garp* was being shot on Manhattan's lower east side.

"They had all these extras," he said, "and some of the extras were supposed to be winos, kind of elegant—they leaned up against the wall but they caught their head at just the right camera angle. And at one point a real wino showed up and started to whiz on the wall."

Robin immediately became the assistant director. "That's not in the film!" he shrieked.

Then, instantly, he was the second assistant director: "Can I help you?" he asked the wino snootily. "What union are you in?"

Then Robin was the wino, jumping up and facing the wall of the Drake Hotel, talking back over his shoulder arrogantly. "I don't need no damned union ____ on your damned film."

Robin (assistant director again): "Jesus, get him out of here!"

Unfortunately, when the movie opened in July 1982— a long time after it had been shot and edited—it was not received enthusiastically, though the reviews were mixed. Probably, Robin suffered most; as the star, he was the main target for the critics.

David Ansen at *Newsweek* laid the film to rest with a typical reviewer's bon mot: "A lot of people felt that *Garp* couldn't be made into a movie. A lot of people were right."

Richard Schickel of *Time* magazine zeroed in on Robin: "Robin Williams's Garp is strictly from Ork; he appears to be visiting his role rather than inhabiting it."

Michael Sragow of *Rolling Stone* liked Glenn Close and John Lithgow, but not Robin's concept of Garp: "George Roy Hill probably picked Robin Williams to play Garp because he's always been such a 'nice' comedian, whose normal moonstruck expression suggests an errant imagination. But Williams doesn't begin to express Garp's strength and complexity; he's most at ease playing Mork-like games with his children."

The World According to Garp, incidentally, was produced by Dodi Al-Fayed, who died in an automobile crash with Princess Diana of England in August 1997. Fayed was also a coproducer of Robin Williams's film *Hook*.

Nothing could have been farther apart than Robin's roles in *Popeye* and *The World According to Garp*. Popeye was strictly a cartoon strip; the dialogue was minimal, and action was all that counted. Garp turned out to be a real chore for Williams; he had to reach inside himself for certain emotional reactions and motivations.

There was at least one similarity, though: George Roy Hill, like Altman, banned improvisation. This caused Williams some trouble at first. But as soon as he caught on to the general pacing of the work, he was able to get along without entertaining the rest of the cast and crew.

In fact, as he realized later, his whole attitude toward the script had changed. At first, he had assumed that dialogue was nothing more than an approximation of what he was going to say. Hill's ban had taught him to think more deeply about the words he was saying, trying to get them to work as the writer had intended.

Once he settled down into the role of Garp, Robin realized that what he had really needed was some kind of dramatic challenge, and he felt he could honestly say that in this picture he had recognized the challenge and taken it up.

Popeye was a muscular fighter. In modern terms, he was a guy with street smarts and plenty of muscle to back them up. Garp, on the other hand, was something of a wimp. He had been born into a world peopled almost exclusively by feminists, so, essentially, he was an alien. The absurd things that happen in *Garp* defy any rational explanation but somehow this doesn't matter, because he is a victim of the fate that is waiting to turn his life into ruins at any moment. And yet Garp is a sympathetic character—not at all the kind of nerd one would expect in the role of loser.

That Garp is not a loser comes through in Robin's insight into the role. It is, in fact, the most noticeable thing about his concept of Garp.

There were some critics who liked *Garp* and respected Robin for his work in it. But Robin's movie career was not developing as he had hoped it would, and again he did what he had done before: he spent his time honing his standup persona and trying out new routines for the comedy clubs.

With the role of Garp, he had been able to see a story both as serious drama and as black comedy. His ability to shift seamlessly from one to the other was something to marvel at. So Robin had moved a giant step forward in his career, but he did not see this at the time, nor did anyone else. It would be some time before anyone noticed exactly what had happened.

Cold Turkey

Everybody's life has turning points, crucial moments when a person reacts to a rigorous shock. As a result, there is a sudden self-reevaluation, a decision, a marked change in one's day-to-day actions.

A turning point in the life of Robin Williams occurred in early March 1982. It was part of a larger crisis that continued through the early months of that year.

Williams's state of mind in early 1982 was largely a result of the success of *Mork and Mindy*, which had catapulted him from obscurity into fame and wealth. As the paychecks rolled in, his physical appearance began to alter. He put on weight and looked pudgy and washed out. Williams always joked that his change in appearance was caused by "vodka and lime juice," but it was much more than that. It was overeating—in general, over-indulging—and also overperforming and over-working.

Later on, he summarized his lifestyle of

that period: "To say that you do just a little cocaine is like saying you're swimming with just a small shark. The biggest mistake is trying to go to bed. You're lying there in a pool of your own sweat, with Buddy Rich pounding on your chest. And if you try to go outside, every bird and animal knows you're fucked up. Inside, you're like a vampire on day shift. Cocaine is God's way of saying you're making too much money."

He was also straining himself physically by over-performing. "I used to go to two or three clubs a night and then go to four or five people's houses, just keeping going, going, going. Maybe get a little sleep, but that didn't matter. The myth of living fast and dying young affected me."

In addition, a side of Robin Williams's life that had been somewhat shaky from the start was now facing a collapse. This was his marriage to Valerie Velardi. Yes, she was still keeping up with him, taking notes on his standup routines, going over the tapes, correcting his flubs, making suggestions, working for the filming company when he was shooting a picture—in short, doing all the things she had been doing all along. But this wasn't enough to keep the marriage going.

Exhausted, she would leave him as he began one of his long nights out; and when he'd finally get home, he'd find her sleeping. Then he'd go to bed and not see her until later the next day. Things were unraveling, but Robin was so wrapped up in himself and his high living that he didn't even seem to notice it.

Now came a new development in their relationship. Valerie, who was already in a mood of self-examination, suddenly found that she had special news for her husband—news that might at one time have been exciting but in their present circumstances might be alarming for him, as well as for her. She was pregnant.

Robin took the news as Valerie had hoped he would: he was elated. But at the same time, he was frightened and unnerved by the prospect of changing his lifestyle to cope with this new situation.

Performing was still the main thing that Robin depended upon to keep him going, to keep his batteries charged, to keep him in fine fettle for his work on television and in the films he was making. But it was taking too much out of him. He was actually unhealthy, even though he did keep going at the astounding pace he had set for himself.

Garp had been an eye-opener for him, though. In fact, Robin gave credit to George Roy Hill for teaching him how to pace himself, not only in his speech patterns but also in his lifestyle.

"*Garp* was a very relaxing and humanizing experience," he said. "It mainly forced me to slow down."

Also, in spite of the hard work involved in *Mork and Mindy*, there were advantages. One of them was the casting of Jonathan Winters as Mork's son. Winters's presence on the set brought in lots of comedians, including Don Novello, who created "Father Guido Sarducci" on *Saturday Night Live*; he and Robin became fast friends. John

Belushi happened to be working with Novello at the time, and he, too, appeared on the set to watch Winters work.

John Belushi was one of the stars of *Saturday Night Live* at its inception. He had also starred in a number of pictures: *Goin' South* (1978); *National Lampoon's Animal House* (1978); *Old Boyfriends* (1979); *1941* (1979); *The Blues Brothers* (1980); *Continental Divide* (1981); and *Neighbors* (1981). He and Robin Williams struck up a friendship from the beginning, though it was casual.

"The best day was when John came by the set and we sat and watched Jonathan Winters, just like two little kids," Robin recalled.

Four months later, on March 5, 1982, Robin Williams dropped in on John Belushi at his rented Chateau Marmont bungalow on Sunset Strip behind the Marmont Hotel.

On the surface everything was as usual—all kinds of entertainment, including drugs. The party was a mix of a few comedians and friends. Belushi was a bit quieter than usual. Robin Williams liked what he saw in Belushi—the two seemed to be "kindred spirits." If these kindred spirits were meant to be friends, then Robin would enter into the relationship wholeheartedly, and so he snorted a line of coke with Belushi that night. "Cocaine for me," Robin attested later, "was a place to hide. Most people get hyper on coke. It slowed me down."

In his book *Wired*, a biography of John Belushi, Bob Woodward describes the scene. John got up for some cocaine, which he took himself and also offered to his guest, Robin Williams. Then Belushi slumped down in a chair. Woodward wrote that his head just dropped, as if he had passed out.

It was a good five minutes before he lifted his head again. Robin was puzzled. What was Belushi up to? According to Woodward, Robin even asked the obvious question: "What's up?" Robin had never seen anyone go out like a light the way Belushi had and then come back so quickly. Somehow, Belushi didn't look well. "Are you okay?" Robin asked tentatively.

"Yeah," Belushi told Robin. "Took a couple of 'ludes.''

But, according to Woodward, he seemed to be more or less frozen there in the chair, as if he were on the edge of sleep.

As it turned out, Robin was almost the last person to see John Belushi alive. Soon after this, Robin left the party. It was late when he got home, and the next day he had to be at the studio to tape *Mork and Mindy*. He managed to get there on time, but he did not notice the wary glances that were cast in his direction by almost everybody on the set.

After the day's scenes were taped, Pam Dawber drew him aside. "Your friend is dead," she told him. Robin had no hint of disaster. He asked which friend, and she told him. John Belushi had been blown away by a speedball just a few hours after Robin had left him.

"I was just getting to know the man!" Robin said

slowly, the shock having unnerved him. "If I had known something was going on, I would have helped him. But nobody knew—myself included."

Robin was crushed by the news. Later on he looked at the situation in a slightly different way, more distanced, more objective, more logical.

"The Belushi tragedy was frightening," he recalled. "He was the strongest. A bull with incredible energy. His death scared a whole group of show business people. It caused a big exodus from drugs."

Later on Robin said, "What really cleaned me up, though, was when I realized I was going to have a child and I thought, I don't want to have a life where I'm not totally aware and ready to go; I don't want to be there. I don't want to live like some strange marsupial ferret, going 'daylight' like a vampire on a day pass."

Yet he knew that he should not have been surprised at what had happened. Belushi was living on the edge— just like Williams himself. And Robin suddenly saw the truth: He was headed in the same direction as John Belushi.

The next few days were strange ones for Robin. For once he stopped thinking about comedy routines and jokes and thought about himself and about his life, in great detail. Looking at himself objectively, he was astounded at how far he had been deviating from the straight line he thought he was following. He realized that he was straying into unknown territory, from which it would be hard to work his way back to the safe and sane life he had once led.

With his world caving in on him, and with the news that he was going to be a father, Robin Williams came to a hard decision. He knew what he had to do. He could do it, and he would. Not many people could succeed at what he planned to do, but *he* could. He was going to stop drugs and liquor cold turkey.

"No visit to the Betty Ford Center, no therapeutic support," a friend said of Robin's action. "He just quit, and he never touched drugs or drink again."

Valerie: "Robin has an incredibly strong will. He didn't need help. He has inner resources and he used them."

Robin had simply gone back to his origins; he knew he could do this if he willed himself to do it. And that was exactly the turn he took. He had read the books. He knew how tough it would be. But he had made his mind up. He managed it. After all, he once pointed out, his mother had been brought up as a Christian Scientist, believing in "mind over matter."

When he did stop drugs and alcohol, he knew he was through with them for life. "For me there was the baby coming. I knew I couldn't be a father and live that sort of life."

This did not mean, however, that his life had straightened out completely. Garp's "undertoad" must have been at work. Suddenly, with the impersonal arrogance of fate, the ax fell at ABC-TV.

In May 1982, *Mork and Mindy* was canceled by the network. The last show was broadcast on June 10, 1982. Robin Williams found himself without his usual weekly pay of $40,000. Not only that, he was incensed at the killing of a successful program and also felt responsible for its death. If he had fought harder for his concepts, perhaps it might have survived for another season.

Of course, the studio had to pay him part of the remainder of the money it owed him for the fifth year of his contract, which had now been abrogated, but the disappearance of the show was a blow that money could not make up for.

John Belushi's death in March and the death of *Mork and Mindy* in May seemed to be linked, and to be a message of some kind. Robin had reacted to Belushi's death by stopping drugs; now he could get out of the "mondo Hollywood" ring.

He had put some money into a six-hundred-acre ranch in Marin County, the wine country north of San Francisco. Now he could leave his house in Topango Canyon and move north—he had always felt better at some distance from the world of Los Angeles. He'd keep the Topango Canyon house and his Hollywood apartment for the future.

Meanwhile, his agency was hard at work looking for projects for him; and *Garp*, despite the generally negative reviews, did better than expected at the box office after it opened in September 1982.

In the fall of 1982, Robin Williams told a magazine writer: "I look back now and see how lucky I was, after the last hectic years in Hollywood, to have *Garp* come along when it did. It was like going from Marvel Comics to Tolstoy."

On September 29, 1982, Robin Williams testified before a grand jury on the death of John Belushi by a drug overdose. No further action was ever taken on the matter.

Robin was now looking for work, though with the demise of *Mork and Mindy* still so recent, he and his agency decided that it would be almost impossible to get something right away. For one thing, the public would expect another alien from Robin Williams, or a fantasy character of some other kind, rather than a real person. Second, anything he chose might remind the public of Mork, and that wouldn't do at all.

Because of his success in creating a brand-new TV character, Robin had become typecast. The trouble was that his type was so original that there were no other shows he could go to. He was not wanted as just another character in a typical sitcom.

Still, the occasional positive reviews of *The World According to Garp* gave the agency an opportunity to seek out slightly offkey roles for Robin, and thus the film *The Survivors* evolved.

Its director, Michael Ritchie, had made several earlier films, some very good and some mediocre, including *Smile* (very, very good), *Downhill Racer* (good), *The Bad News Bears* (okay), and *Semi-Tough* (so-so). The script was written by Michael Leeson, whose scripts for the television series *Taxi* had won a number of awards.

The basic theme of *The Survivors* is how to survive in a society that does not allow an average decent man to come through his life unscathed by fate. Its opening could almost have been written in the 1990s: it starts with downsizing at the firm where Donald Quinelle—the role Robin Williams was to play—works as a junior executive. The sequence is a quick wrap: Quinelle is fired summarily and told to clear out his desk and leave the premises immediately.

At almost the same moment, Sonny Paluso, played by Walter Matthau, loses the gas station that is his primary occupation. He, too, is a victim of downsizing. These two dissimilar people wander around in a state of shock, and the story gets moving when they meet in a diner, where they grouse about their bad luck.

Then, a masked gunman (played by Jerry Reed) enters the diner and tries to rob the proprietor. By now, Donald is so turned off by the rotten world—and his own bad luck—that he erupts like a geyser, something that he has never done before. He chews out the would-be holdup man to such a degree that both the gunman and Sonny are startled. The slow-moving, grousing Sonny comes to Donald's aid, and the two unlikely heroes disarm the bandit, who is arrested. Sonny and Donald, ogled by TV cameras, become instant media celebrities.

"I'll get you yet!" threatens the would-be robber as he is led away, shaking and rattling his handcuffs.

After this promising beginning, however, the film meanders away from satire to melodrama. The episode has caused Donald to reevaluate his position in life and reinvent himself in a dramatic way. No longer will he be a white-collar nerd. He will be a gun-toting hero, as in a Western, shooting down the bad guys who seem to inhabit most of his universe. He enrolls in a course in survival tactics at a camp in New England.

Sonny follows him, unable to believe that this meek, mild clerk has become a raving gun nut—for Donald's next move is to get an arsenal to protect himself from retaliation by the coffee-shop bandit.

When the robber, whose name is Jack, is released from prison, he does go after Donald and Sonny. Comedy predominates here, with Robin playing in his usual semi-crazed style, and Matthau in his sour-faced cynical style. There is a problem here, since Matthau's type of humor doesn't play well against Robin's. They are out of sync with each other.

Richard Schickel reviewed the film for *Time*, saying this about Robin Williams's role: "Michael Leeson, who wrote scripts for the TV series *Taxi*, uses that show's mixture of urban gallantry and paranoia in his first feature. He has given Williams his best chance to vent his singular, hysterical style in a movie and provided Matthau, stooped and shuffling under the burden of his sanity, with his richest part in years."

Pauline Kael wrote in the *New Yorker*: "The best thing about this framework is that it permits Robin Williams to be himself and yet to be Donald. He acts with an emotional purity that I can't pretend to understand.''

Vincent Canby said: "Mr. Williams does a number of his hysterical, overwrought comedy turns that don't easily fit into the comparatively straight comedy that Mr. Matthau is playing.''

Although Pauline Kael was enthusiastic, the picture opened without any signs of success and soon vanished from the scene. The problem seems to have been its rather uneasy combination of downsizing and right-wing terrorism.

The comedic elements of the story line had seemed flawless on paper, but by the time they were transposed to film, the laughs, if any, were more stifled than robust. The general sense was that the film was just next door to a flop. Leonard Maltin, in his *Movie and Video Guide*, gave it two stars, which promises to relegate this movie to the dusty shelves of video stores.

The movie's shortcomings are evident in any honest appraisal. The script calls for a complete change of character in Donald. Indeed, Sonny can be observed casting seemingly casual glances at his companion in arms for a possible revelation, but that revelation never comes. And the total change at the end is simply unbelievable as Robin plays it. In fact, neither the lead nor the second lead can stand up to the test of logic. The story becomes almost a satire of itself as the nerd becomes a John Wayne hero and Sonny becomes one of the Marx Brothers. It is a melodramatic meltdown, not character development.

Knowing what Robin Williams was going through in his private life at the time he made *The Survivors* helps viewers understand some of his moves: as he was struggling with his own persona, he was also struggling with the persona of Donald. In the end, Robin never did sort things out in his own mind before he took on the task of conveying the change from inaction to action demanded by this role. It seems obvious, from what we see on the screen, that Robin was still being hounded by his own misgivings and bedeviled by his fear that he had lost his way.

In truth, he had lost his way professionally, at least for the time being. It would take almost a miracle to bring him back to the path he had been following so assiduously.

"Just Be Daddy"

Chapter Six

The big event in Robin Williams's life in 1983 was the birth of his son, Zachary. In fact, this addition to the family helped consolidate both Robin and Valerie in their roles of husband and wife as well as father and mother. Up to the point when Robin had sworn off drugs and liquor the marriage was in trouble, drifting but headed for oblivion.

Robin was womanizing. When his big break came in *Mork and Mindy*, he had decided that women were a wonderful thing for him to spend his time on. And the women were all there waiting for him.

"For many years," he later admitted, "I was addicted to women, as if to a drug. That's over now. But looking back, I find it humiliating. Degrading. I'm ashamed."

Valerie was trying to understand. "Very attractive women threw themselves at men in his position. You'd have to be a saint to resist. Besides, neither of us was prepared for the sudden life shift. But I admit the other women were harder to take after I'd had a child."

Luckily, it was then that Robin began to settle down into a new life pattern. His agency got him an interesting new picture to work on, *Moscow on the Hudson*, about a musician defector and his adventures in New York City.

The energy Robin had used in his womanizing and in his late-night performances was now channeled into volcanic creativity. The new project would take a great deal of energy—he set himself the daunting goal of learning to speak Russian with a passable accent. He also took saxophone lessons, since the character was a saxophonist.

Most of his friends supported his new attitude toward life. In fact, they told him he was much more "centered" than he had been before.

Robin's response: "Sounds as if eventually I'll just be a dot."

Christopher Reeve, his classmate at Juilliard, had kept in touch, and he liked the change in Robin. "He's discovered that he doesn't need to be on all the time to be close to people. He used to think his gift was all he had to give."

Robin's change of pace began to get his creative juices flowing. "I take more down time," he said. "Catatonic time when I'm absorbing information. People say I'm absorbent—makes me think I'm a giant Tampax." And his sense of propriety and his sense of priorities had improved. He listened, he evaluated, and he made constructive choices more quickly and accurately. *Moscow on the Hudson* was one such choice. And in the end it paid off—to a degree, at least.

Robin was now spending a great deal of his time with

Zachary. The arrival of a son was the greatest thing Robin had experienced in his life.

"In the morning, I often watch TV with Zach. They show those wonderful old Warner Bros. cartoons. To hear a child laugh like that—to see him watch Wile E. Coyote! My God, it's something incredible! Sometimes while the cartoons are showing I do wacky voices—you know, the way I do in my act. Sometimes he likes that, but sometimes he says, 'Daddy, don't use that voice. Just be Daddy.' And that's what I want to do. Just be Daddy."

The film Robin made shortly after *The Survivors* was very much out of the general run of his pictures. That is, in *Moscow on the Hudson*—unlike *Popeye*, *The World According to Garp*, or *The Survivors*—there were no elements of comedy behind the story line.

Moscow was essentially a simple story: a Russian musician defects to America. It was simplistic because the defection turns out to be a spur-of-the-moment thing, and its result is pretty much all happiness for the defector. Essentially, there were none of the factors contributing to real-life defections.

The story was written by Paul Mazursky and Leon Capetanos. This was to be a Mazursky-type production, typical of the man responsible for *Bob and Carol and Ted and Alice* (1969), *Blume in Love* (1973), *Harry and Tonto* (1974), and *An Unmarried Woman* (1978), to name a few. The story was divided into two parts: events leading up to the defection, and events flowing from the defection.

Robin Williams was cast as the protagonist, Vladimir

Ivanoff, a Russian saxophonist in a band that accompanies a performing circus. His day-to-day life in Moscow is a dreary study in survivorship. He lives in a crowded apartment with three generations of his family, including his grandfather, whom he worships (the man has a sense of humor, and because of that is Vladimir's favorite relative).

His sex life is hardly fulfilling; he and his girlfriend have to borrow a friend's apartment. The girlfriend hounds him about joining the Communist party, but Vladimir is an independent spirit who loves the idea of freedom—no party stuff for him. His buddy Anatoly, played by Elya Baskin, is the circus clown. Anatoly, astounds Vlad when he confides in him that he's going to defect in America on the circus's next trip to New York.

Vladimir doesn't believe Anatoly but does his best to talk him out of this crazy notion, pointing out to his friend that he is bound to notify the KGB agents who accompany the circus that Anatoly will be taking off. But it's just a threat; he doesn't mean it.

The big scene takes place in Bloomingdale's. The circus performers are bussed to the store, where they are allowed an hour to shop. It is here that the crucial action takes place. Anatoly loses his nerve and sheepishly leaves the store with the other circus people. Vladimir, annoyed by the KGB agents, who are watching everybody closely, hides himself and surrenders as a defector to a Bloomingdale's security guard, who offers Vladimir a place to live.

In order to give the film some reality, the scenes in Russia and some in New York are spoken in Russian with

English subtitles. Robin Williams certainly sounds Russian, at least to most American viewers, and the subtitles make more sense than those in some foreign films.

In spite of the momentum created by the first half of the film, the second half bogs down. Vlad—as the Americans call him—becomes involved with the Bloomingdale's salesclerk who helped him hide when he defected. (She is played by Maria Conchita Alonso, a Venezuelan actress.)

But the affair soon runs off the track. Through a letter delivered by another Russian, Vlad learns that his grandfather has died. Eventually, Vlad is mugged on his way home. He fights back but simply gets beaten up.

One of the problems with this film is that it just peters out. A supposedly rousing last scene—in a restaurant where a number of New York ethnics start to recite the Declaration of Independence—strikes one as a bit of hokum, added simply to repeat the overall theme, which doesn't really need repeating.

Robin Williams was pleased with the job he did in the film. "I think it's my best all-around film so far," he told a reporter for the *New York Times*. "I worked harder on it than I ever worked on a film. I would prepare for every scene the night before, so that when I came in to do it, I came in ready."

One of his hardest jobs was learning to speak Russian correctly, so that his diction would not offend Russian viewers. "I studied five hours a day every day for three months," he said. "It was just like a Berlitz course."

An even tougher task was learning to play the saxophone, so that he wouldn't look as if he were faking it on camera. "The hardest was playing the saxophone, because I had never played an instrument before." Robin studied under Greg Phillips, a saxophonist from San Francisco, two hours a day for about eight months before the filming of *Moscow on the Hudson* began in New York. "I started out awful, but I got to be okay. I was really playing in all the scenes, but eventually it was overdubbed, because I only studied for such a short time. But I still play—I play soprano sax and my wife plays flute. We play Mozart concertos together."

Once again, on the set of *Moscow on the Hudson* Robin did not play the same kind of off-camera role he had played on *Mork and Mindy*, entertaining the troops with free-association comedy routines off the top of his head. It was difficult for him to keep from "slipping out of the role" of Vladimir, so he "sort of submerged and isolated" himself from the rest of the cast and the crew. "I suppose they thought I was moody," he noted, "but I think they understood."

He did have a role model for this part: a man named Vlad West, a New York saxophonist who had emigrated from Russia. Not only Vlad West's personality went into the film, Robin pointed out. In West's East Village apartment there were shower curtains with an American flag pattern, and the film's art director used this element in Vladimir Ivanoff's apartment. But there was more to the character than just Vlad West. Robin also incorporated elements of his language teacher, David Gomburg, and most of the character he pulled up from "various parts" of himself.

Robin got a lot of ideas from talking to Russian-born actors hired to do scenes in Munich, where the picture's Moscow scenes were shot on location. "Many of them were actors or directors in Russia, and now most of them work for Radio Free Europe. They're the ones who told me I sounded like a real Russian, or if not that, a Czech or a Pole."

It was thought that perhaps the film tended to make life in Moscow look too bleak, impossible for the average person to stomach. "I take it from a personal view," Robin said, "that the thing that makes this country interesting is the people. I think a lot of Americans have lost track that we all basically come from that route."

Nevertheless, there is an almost surreal quality to the picture that keeps you watching it, and most of it is supplied by the acting of Robin Williams.

Pauline Kael loved Robin's performance in *Moscow*. She called the general effect "Chaplinesque."

Richard Schickel wrote in *Time:* "The store scene is wonderful, a perfect paradigm of the kind of tangled wrangle no true New Yorker can resist joining. . . . Thereafter, though, the film loses its verve." He liked Robin Williams: "Robin Williams, who seems to have absorbed something of the Russian soul while acquiring a persuasive Russian accent, is excellent. He provides all the sweetness any picture needs."

Newsweek reported: "The good news about *Moscow on the Hudson* is the surprising ease with which Robin Williams enters the skin of this confused, ambitious, melancholy Russian. . . . The bad news is that once Mazursky and his cowriter, Leon Capetanos, set their hero loose in Manhattan . . . they don't know what to do with him."

Now, some ten years after the fall of the Berlin wall and the end of the era of defections to the West by Russian artists, writers, and athletes, Vladimir Ivanoff is somewhat an anomaly. Yet in 1984, when the film opened in America, defection was still very much alive. At that time, of course, most literary defections were used as a plot device to move a spy story forward. It was in this regard that Robin Williams's role was important: his was a more realistic approach to defection.

The absence of melodrama and shootouts made *Moscow* a delight for the more astute moviegoer, as most of the critics noted. And Robin's preparation for the role also gave it a particularly realistic quality. This realism was not gritty but rather a genuine empathy with the character.

Unerringly, Robin had chosen the kind of role he loved to do in those days. Vlad was a stranger in a strange land, trying to cope with all the problems that an alien would face in a new world.

The action was very real, but it was gentle. The defection was portrayed as a duel of wits—vocal rather than muscular. One could almost feel the way Robin was feeling as he played this role.

Thus *Moscow* was another step forward, and a success, in the career of Robin Williams. Through his friendly, straightforward playing, he was able to bring the audience into complete rapport with Vlad. The suspense engendered was a matter of wondering what would happen next to Vlad, rather than a chase and capture of a defector.

Robin has said that he reached down into himself for various elements of the character of Vlad. But he was also serious about learning to speak Russian, and about his extensive work with the saxophone.

The public, except in a few rare cases, might not have recognized this role as a step forward, and *Moscow on the Hudson* was in fact soon shunted aside as just a "nice try" by a rising star. But it provided evidence that Robin Williams might soon break out into something that would make everyone sit up and take notice.

Marking Time

While Robin worked on his career, his home life had improved dramatically. He was happier living in San Francisco than in Los Angeles—he rented an apartment in San Francisco and owned the ranch in Marin County—and everything was looking up, except, of course, in the one most important area.

Valerie was still trying to do her job as Robin's assistant in his comedy work, but the arrival of Zachary had complicated her day-to-day routine. And so the two of them finally decided that it would be expedient—even necessary—to hire a live-in nanny.

There were also misunderstandings between them—misunderstandings that continued to make their life together less than satisfactory. And as these misunderstandings escalated, they tended to upset Zachary, who seemed always to be in the middle of the confrontations.

In turn, young Zachary began showing evidence of a troubled psyche. What was happening was a circular effect: as Zachary's presence inflamed the Williamses, their own hostilities increased the tension within their son.

In 1984 the Williamses hired Marsha Garces, a woman in her middle twenties, to take care of Zachary. Zachary had become a real handful by then, but the new nanny seemed to be able to shoulder the burden without too much trouble.

Marsha was of Filipino-Finnish descent. Her father, Leon Garces, was a chef. He had been born in Cebu, in the Philippines, and had spent two years in medical school at the University of the Philippines before immigrating to the United States. Marsha's mother, Ina, was the daughter of immigrants who lived on a farm in Owen, Wisconsin, about two hundred miles from Milwaukee.

Marsha had been trained in her early years as a painter, but because she was not successful at that trade, she had taken turns as a waitress and other odd jobs that might come along. "I grew up in a German community," she said, "where all the other kids were blond, and we were dark, so I know what it feels like to be what is considered different." She was different from her brother and sisters, too: they were social; she was a loner. She became a voracious reader during her childhood.

Marsha decided that Milwaukee was not the place for her and went west, taking art classes at San Francisco State College and working as a waitress at night. Finally she got a job as a bank supervisor, but the job bored her; she went back to waitressing. "I learned that I had an instinct for making people feel comfortable." Before being hired by the Williamses, she had been married and divorced twice. At the time she was hired, she was involved in another serious relationship.

Working for the Williamses, Marsha settled down. "I'm proud of how well I cared for him," she said later on. "I loved Zach." Soon, Marsha was handling more than Zachary. She began to take over some of the work that Valerie had been doing—working as Robin's assistant, organizing and arranging his tours, taking care of his fan mail, and so on.

By 1986, she had become Robin's secretary. The relationship between Valerie and Robin was by then in shambles. Valerie was on her own, as she herself described it, and things were going badly with the Williams family. There were stormy sessions between Robin and Valerie— usually over Zachary, but sometimes involving Marsha as well.

In late 1987, Robin and Valerie signed a private agreement to separate. They had already been living apart for a long time, but now it was legal. The agreement provided for joint custody of Zachary, on a more or less flexible basis.

When Robin was out of town, as he often was, their son lived with Valerie in her San Francisco apartment. When Robin was at home in another part of the city,

Zachary spent as much time as possible with him. And of course when Zachary was with Robin, he was with Marsha, too. She and Robin were living together by this time, and she was acting both as his secretary-assistant and as his most significant other.

But basically Robin's life was becoming centered on Zachary. By the time Robin and Valerie separated, Robin was talking to the press about his love for Zachary. "He's just wonderful! The most sobering and wonderful thing in my life. Blond. Valerie's blue eyes. My chin. Full lips. He looks like an Aryan poster child. He has a very fertile imagination and he loves numbers. Sometimes he's like an angel without wings. He knows what he's feeling at all times."

The separation arrangement between Robin and Valerie seemed to be working out with regard to their son. "He's amazingly adaptive," Robin observed, "and we all try hard to make the arrangement work. We all love Zachary, and Zachary loves us all. Also, we're all in therapy, and that's helped a lot. Jesus! I should get a discount!"

Valerie agreed that Robin was handling things nicely. "Robin has been conducting himself very well. We're acting together in Zach's interest. We separated to reexamine our lives. It's a time for personal growth for both of us. I see another man, but I live alone, and I like it that way." The "other man" was David Sheff, a journalist.

But Robin was never insensitive to the problems that developed in the arrangement. "The problem is intensified because Zachary loves Marsha and Marsha loves the child.

So for Valerie, along with the feeling that Marsha took me away, there's the threat that Marsha might replace her in Zach's affections. That won't happen."

While Robin was trying to make sense of his stressful family life, he made a couple of theatrical films and played in a television drama. He was still seeking a breakthrough movie—one that would put him at the top of the heap. After all, he had managed to be at the top of the television heap. Why couldn't he be at the top of the film heap?

The first of these films was another change of pace for Robin Williams. It was a sports film, called *The Best of Times*; the scriptwriter was Ron Shelton, and the director was Roger Spottiswoode. Shelton once called it "a soufflé flipped like a Frisbee."

It was an attempt on the part of the filmmakers to do something like one of the small-town pix of the 1930s, such as Preston Sturges's *Hail the Conquering Hero* or *The Miracle of Morgan's Creek*. In this case the small town was Taft, California (population 5,000), whose rivalry with Bakersfield (population 100,000), just down the road, formed the nexus of the plot.

Thirteen years ago, Jack Dundee (played by Robin Williams) fumbled a touchdown pass from the high school's star quarterback, Reno Hightower (played by Kurt Russell), and Dundee has been branded a fumblefingers from that day on. He's tired of bearing all this shame. On a visit to his friendly hooker, he gripes about it. She suggests that he play a rematch, and so he does.

The story focuses on the two couples, the Jack Dundees and the Reno Hightowers, as Jack feverishly tries to manipulate the reluctant Reno into backing the idea of a rematch with Bakersfield. Nobody really wants the thing to take place, except Jack; and he makes everybody suffer along with him when it does happen.

The plot has a foregone conclusion, of course, and yet everything seems to come off well, with cheers at the end of the piece.

Ralph Novack covered the movie for *People:* "Williams does such an engaging Everyman it's impossible not to root for him, and Russell plays straight man without being upstaged."

Paul Attanasio of the *Washington Post* also focused on Robin Williams: "Williams is a dazzling verbal comedian and an expert mimic (there's a fine scene here where he paints a picture of Reno's former glory with sound effects)."

There was nothing really wrong with *The Best of Times.* It had a strong cast, and the story seemed okay. Yet it just didn't have the makings of a hit. The problem seemed to be that the plot, while simple, was unbelievable. The idea that a onetime football player like Robin Williams's character would restage a game he had lost in the past doesn't quite add up. In addition, Jack Dundee is a faceless, bodyless oddball rather than a sharply focused individual. Even with a few attempts at standup riffs by Robin Williams in a scene or two, the picture never seems to grab hold of the audience.

The climax of the picture is the replaying of the football game, but that, too, seems unfocused. The actors seem to be trying to come up with what the dialogue and the script call for, but they never get it under control—and that includes Williams and Kurt Russell.

The second theatrical film was a quiet, unpretentious little comedy called *Club Paradise*. As might be guessed from the title, it was a visit to the very popular Club Med in the Caribbean during the 1980s. This film was directed by Harold Ramis, who was known for his comedies and had been the director of *National Lampoon's Vacation*.

The loose-jointed script was by Brian Doyle-Murray, but a number of other writers had a part in getting the story to the point where Doyle-Murray began working on it—and when the actors were cast, they were encouraged to come up with their own gags and dialogue. Of course, there was nothing new in this for Robin Williams, who always managed to come up with his own gags—whether they were used or not—when he did any film.

There isn't much to the story except the jokes, but there is a semblance of a plot. Jack Moniker (played by Robin Williams) is a fireman in Chicago. One day, half a building falls on top of him. He wins a big insurance settlement and decides to invest the money in a buddy's idea of running a beach resort along the lines of Club Med in the Caribbean. Ernest (played by Jimmy Cliff) buys a run-down resort on an island and opens it, expecting a deluge of guests.

The guests are mostly comedians from *Saturday Night*

Live and other TV shows, each with his or her own brand of slapstick humor. In addition, there are Twiggy, the British model, who becomes Robin's girlfriend, and Joanna Cassidy, who becomes the girlfriend of Peter O'Toole, the British governor of the island.

Club Paradise is hardly a paradise. It was a decadent resort, and the remodeling has failed to improve it. Also, the "bad guys" on the island want to develop a ritzy establishment with a king-size hotel overlooking the beachfront, right where Club Paradise is.

Gags flow freely from everybody on the set. Robin Williams manages to get his yucks by using a kind of dry high-comedy delivery. For example, when a racist visitor begins to talk about the "good old days" of slavery, when productivity was high, Williams retorts: "Yeah, a good day's work for a good day's beating." When a hungry group of resort guests come across a field of sugarcane, Andrea Martin vows: "I'm not about to eat *real* sugar." Eugene Levy snorts: "All right, fine. We'll find you a Sweet'n Low field."

At the end, the good guys and the bad guys tangle in a confrontation scene that features Peter O'Toole in a hilarious role as peacemaker. He does make peace, and he saves Club Paradise for the people who have discovered it for what it's worth.

The next picture that Robin Williams made during this time was a dramatic adaptation of a Saul Bellow novella, *Seize the Day*. Because it was first broadcast on television and was not shown in a regular motion picture theater, it has been categorized as a "made for TV" drama rather than a theatrical film.

The reason it was not premiered in theaters had to do with Robin Williams and his agents. The picture was definitely a downer—the story of a man in the worst period of his life. Downers do not usually generate much sympathy from moviegoers, and it was felt that if the picture opened in a theater the box-office ratings would be quite low and would not make Robin Williams attractive for future movies.

The shooting script was adapted from the novella by Ronald Ribman, and the film was directed by Fielder Cook. It is the story of a fortyish man named Tommy Wilhelm, a man facing oblivion—down and out in Manhattan.

Tommy Wilhelm (played by Robin Williams) is a failed actor who became a salesman to make ends meet but has now lost even that last-ditch job. He has also walked out on his wife, who has refused to give him a divorce but won't live with him either. His grown-up kids won't speak to him.

A friend advised Wilhelm to invest in the commodities market. He did so, and the money is gone. In fact, almost all his money is gone. He can't get work. He can't get anything together anymore. He is on the verge of a nervous breakdown.

He has moved into a seedy old hotel on Manhattan's upper Broadway, where he is surrounded by a lot of old people—among them his father, who considers him a loser and doesn't hate him but simply ignores him.

Tommy has taken up with another woman, and she is pestering him to get a divorce from his wife and marry her. Everything is going to hell for him.

The story involves Tommy's attempts to hold things together long enough so he can get back to work and straighten himself out. But no one is there to help him do even that. He had fallen through the bottom of a hole in the earth.

The majority of the reviews of *Seize the Day* were highly complimentary to Robin Williams and to the film itself—but not so the *New York Times*'s review by John O'Connor, who hated the film and particularly disliked Robin Williams in the role of Tommy Wilhelm: "Mr. Williams is a singularly gifted comic actor and comedian, a master of dizzying improvisation. Unfortunately, his performance in *Seize the Day* is a miscasting fiasco, all the more regrettable because so much intense care has been so obviously spent on the production."

O'Connor pointed out that Williams was physically wrong for the character. He didn't like Williams's acting either, claiming that there was no buildup toward disaster—that disaster was already present in everything Robin Williams did. He also disliked the characterization of Wilhelm's father. At the end of his review, he wrote: "A feasible Tommy Wilhelm would have made all the difference."

Alan Bunce, in the *Christian Science Monitor*, called Robin Williams's performance "remarkable": "It's quite a feat to keep a character anchored somewhere in reality while doing justice to its absurdist potential. It takes an actor full of sharp, deep comic insights but solid enough to be more than a symbol."

Still, it is hard to imagine how Robin Williams might have thought that playing such a role would lift him out of the depths to which he himself had sunk in his run of failures after *Moscow on the Hudson*. Perhaps he felt that it could be a good role for an actor who was beginning to feel at home in straight drama, but there was no question that Saul Bellow's character was one of the grimmest, most depressing, and thoroughly unpleasant he had ever created. Moreover, the script for *Seize the Day* followed the book fairly closely, pushing Tommy further and further down, with every nuance of his life turned into a thorn in his side through morbid reversal after morbid reversal. Thus the film is a relentless procession of defeats and thwarted attempts to get something going right.

Another possibility is that Robin Williams chose the role as a sort of workout. He would be experimenting with all kinds of tics, convulsions, and displays of anguish. The critics, who generally favored Robin Williams, tried to figure out what he had gained by this dangerous experiment, and the consensus was that he simply wanted to show the acting world what he had in the way of talent.

Good Morning, Robin

The words the early-morning disk jockey used were actually "Good morning, Heraklion"—not catchy enough to become a household phrase. This was on the island of Crete in the mid-1960s, and Adrian Cronauer originally used the greeting as he began his morning stint for Armed Forces Radio in Greece.

Cronauer later requested a transfer to Vietnam, and he was shipped there in 1965 to take over as a disk jockey for Armed Forces Radio in Saigon. Feeling that his "Good morning" salutation was a part of him, he continued to use it. Having loosened up his style, he now boomed out the greeting with unrestrained, almost manic, glee; and "Good morning, Vietnam!" became a catchphrase of that misunderstood war.

There was more to Cronauer's stint than the rousing greeting. He also loosened up the radio show itself. He turned the stuffy Armed Forces station sound into something like a stateside radio broadcast. He juiced up the announcements with humor and played Top 40 hits as he had done at home in Arlington, Virginia, at the beginning of his career.

Cronauer did clash occasionally with the military authorities on what news should be presented and what should be eliminated. In the end, he always bowed to the brass. In Vietnam, Cronauer met Ben Moses, another disk jockey for Armed Forces Radio. After a year's hitch in Saigon, Cronauer's service was over and he returned to the States.

A few years later, he was still in radio and television, and still in touch with Moses, who had also gone into television. In 1978, Moses sublet Cronauer's New York apartment. Out of this friendship came an idea for working together.

"We thought that if we put the idea of *M*A*S*H*, which made comedy out of the Korean War, with the idea of *WKRP in Cincinnati*, which made comedy out of broadcasting, we'd have a pilot for a sitcom," Moses said. "I took the idea to ABC in 1978. They said they couldn't *possibly* do anything funny about Vietnam."

Three years later, an agent friend of Moses' suggested that he write the story up as a screen treatment and send it around the studios. "Adrian and I brainstormed, and I wrote a twenty-page treatment." It was still unsuccessful, although it made the usual rounds. The problem was that nobody bit on it.

But in 1983, Larry Brezner, who was Robin Williams's

manager and by then a partner with Rollins, Morra, and Brezner, saw the script and became aware of its possibilities.

Brezner liked the basic idea of the story for a TV pilot, but he didn't like the particular approach the script had taken. He knew it needed a professional writer. And so he hired Mitch Markowitz to work on it. Markowitz had done several good *M*A*S*H* scripts and knew his way around Hollywood.

Brezner and Markowitz worked together to put the script into a more entertaining form. It was a newly typed copy of this script that Robin Williams noticed on Brezner's desk one day. Robin read it and liked it; he thought it had potential.

The script became the basis of the movie *Good Morning, Vietnam*. With Robin Williams involved in the project, Brezner got busy and approached Paramount. However, there was a disagreement between the studio and the principals interested in doing the picture. One of Paramount's producers wanted a kind of "Animal House in Vietnam." Brezner and Williams nixed that idea, and Paramount backed out.

But waiting in the wings was Jeffrey Katzenberg, chairman of Walt Disney Studios. He knew who Robin Williams was and he could envision a great film with Williams in the role of Adrian Cronauer.

"As a movie executive, I had dreamed of seeing what Robin Williams could do presented on the screen some

day. You say to Robin, 'What would you like to drink?'
and he does ten minutes on the state of the world, he tells
you how to bring peace to the world, it's hilarious—and
it's relevant to the drink.'' Katzenberg went on, ''And
Robin's improvisations are at the center of what this movie
is. It is about a disk jockey who gets on the air and goes
through four hours a day of improvisational entertainment, narration, news bulletins, introductions to records.
And those parts would give Robin his chance to improvise.'' Improvisation, of course, was Robin's strong point.

Walt Disney Studios bought the idea and put the picture into production. The concept was tailored to fit the
peculiar talents of Robin Williams; as a result, the picture
became a vehicle where Robin Williams could be funny—
where his free-association approach to mimicry and
standup comedy would be uninhibited by strictures of
script.

Barry Levinson came onboard as the director. He had
already turned out hits like *Diner* and *Tin Men*, and his
talent would probably be the kind to induce Robin to do
his best improvisational work.

What was more, Levinson understood Robin Williams
and could see what problems he would have to deal with
in working with Robin. He could also see the benefits that
should accrue from their combined talents.

''Until this role,'' Levinson said, referring to Robin
Williams's previous attempts to combine comedy and
drama, ''the acting and the comedy have been pretty much

separate onscreen.'' He knew it was the chance to do improvisations that had persuaded Robin to take this role in the first place.

Yet sometimes when they were working together, as Robin later noted, "Barry would say, 'You don't have to be funny here.' In the past I used to think, 'I'll push it; I'll make it funnier.' " Here that was not necessary.

There were some other wrinkles to be ironed out in Levinson and Williams's working relationship. Levinson discovered that Robin, in spite of his professionalism, was intimidated by the closeness of the camera; it put him on guard and made him wary of doing something dumb.

"I tried to take advantage of Robin's amazing mind," Levinson said. "We went after whatever he was doing. I used a longer lens than usual so the camera wasn't on top of him; it wasn't like those shots that are so handsomely composed that the actor can't step out of the light ring. I just let him work."

And work he did. Robin appreciated his director's background. "Barry once was a part of a standup comedy team with Craig T. Nelson, the actor who played the father in *Poltergeist*." (Nelson also played "Coach" in the television show of that name.) "I think that helped us work together. He was willing to let me go. I can think of only two of my lines in the movie that were in the original script."

Levinson once talked about directing and editing those ad-libbed broadcasts of Robin Williams's. "It's like watching a Polaroid come into focus. You say, 'Ooohhh, that's good—but it's not quite there.' And then it starts to emerge, and emerge, and it gets sharper and sharper—and all of a sudden you say, 'Yeah! That's it! We got that!' "

This was just the right working atmosphere to bring out the best in Robin Williams. The script itself, polished by Brezner and Markowitz, left a lot of loose ends for Robin to fill with improvisation. But the true story of Cronauer in Vietnam was only partially told.

For example, the script calls for Cronauer to teach English in a school in Saigon so that he can get to know a Vietnamese girl he has seen in a crowd. Cronauer actually taught English to get to know the Vietnamese people.

In the script, Cronauer meets the girl through her brother, who befriends Cronauer. He continues his relationship with the girl and her brother and is present when a Vietcong bomb blows up a restaurant.

The real Cronauer was also present at a bomb explosion, but when he tried to report it on the radio, he was prevented by the army brass. In the script, Robin Williams makes a big thing out of the censorship and is frustrated by it. This leads to a confrontation between the brass and Cronauer, who is deliberately sent out on a route that is infamous for Vietcong attacks.

But according to Cronauer, "The movie is me trying to play rock and roll and the brass not letting me. That didn't really happen."

Cronauer has also said that he himself was not nearly

as funny as Robin Williams is in the film. "Robin was the me I would have liked to have been. If I had been a little less afraid of courting a court-martial, I probably would have done what he did in the film. I was iconoclastic—but I didn't really get kicked out of Vietnam. I left when my tour of duty was over."

About his loud wake-up greeting, Cronauer said: "I realized that coming on that jubilant might be in bad taste, to say the least. But then I decided there was an element of irony in there. I found out later that on bad days, some of the troops would hear me and turn to their radio and say the GI equivalent of 'Get stuffed, Cronauer!' "

Thanks to Barry Levinson's wide-open style of direction, Robin Williams was able to make more use of his comedic talents than he had ever been permitted to do before—at least in front of motion picture cameras. The film lasts about ninety minutes, and twenty minutes are Robin Williams being himself, a comedian *par excellence* of free association. In fact, this was what made the picture a success—and helped Robin move beyond being an also-ran, the status to which the critics had relegated him in the past.

"I'm putting more of myself into [this picture] than anything I've done before," Robin Williams told Donald Chase in *US* magazine. As Cronauer, he went on, "I'm reacting however I would react to the situation."

When the picture opened, it was billed as the first comedy of the Vietnam War. This annoyed veterans' groups, who immediately said that there was nothing funny about the war and began demonstrations against the film.

Robin Williams was unhappy about the way the picture was promoted at the outset. "I don't want to bust some [veterans'] memories up. I don't want to mock. I want to do something real to them and funny to them."

As it happened, except for the rebuke from veterans' groups—which subsided as soon as the picture began making its mark at the box office—*Good Morning, Vietnam* was a success from its opening day. After its first weekend, in January 1988, it was America's most popular motion picture. This was the hit Robin Williams, along with his fans and his agents, had been waiting for.

Time's Richard Schickel wrote: "The film is the best military comedy since *M*A*S*H* disbanded. The reason is that it is not afraid to work the extremes."

Mike McGrady at *Newsday* wrote: "*Good Morning, Vietnam* gives Robin Williams a role that takes full advantage of his unpredictable genius, and director Barry Levinson knows how to set off the star's unique talent against a believable backdrop."

Robin Williams has talked at length about the picture. Discussing his own role, he said, "There's no character, really. It is myself. It is five percent character and ninety-five percent me, so there's maybe not that effort to keep this character going. When you perform, you are like that. It's BOOM, then you're down."

He said of the movie's politics: ''Nobody on the film had served in Vietnam, except one guy who works for Barry Levinson and used to do secret jungle stuff. Real big guy, kind of scary, can do heavy things. He likes the film. Which is good.''

At one point Robin talked about how hard it had been to get financial backing to make the picture. No one could really understand what the film was about. ''They had a hard time figuring out a comedy set in Vietnam. That's sort of like doing an Inquisition musical. [Throaty singing:] 'I'm gonna wash that blood right out of your eye!' . . . I can't talk too deep about Vietnam. I wasn't there. It's sort of like asking Catfish Hunter about particle acceleration. I've made a movie, that's all.''

Good Morning, Vietnam opened during the Christmas– New Year's season of 1987–1988, playing on only four screens at first but drawing in more crowds than antici- pated. In its limited run it was grossing $1 million a week, a strong showing for a new film. When it was released on a much wider basis in 1988, it grossed over $12 million the first weekend—and the numbers kept growing. By the time its run ended, *Good Morning, Vietnam* had earned $123.9 million in the United States. As one mathemati- cally inclined fan reported to Robin Williams, the picture made as much as the grosses of all seven of Robin's films up to that point.

The critics who liked it were lavish in their praise, and there were enough of them to cause joy in the Robin Williams camp. Even the critics who did not like the film—claiming in most cases that it was just another Robin Williams standup performance—noted that Robin was a giant talent who had finally found his niche.

But the fate that troubled the character Garp—whom Robin had played so well—was also beginning to trouble the actor. While his professional life soared, his personal life began to show evidence of foundering.

About eight weeks before the release of *Good Morning, Vietnam*, Robin Williams was informed by his mother that his father had died.

Thinking about his father, Robin said, "I got to know another side of him in the last few years. I saw that he was funkier, that he had a darker side that made the other side work. He was much older than me; he died at eighty-one.

"Up until four or five years ago, I kept my distance, out of respect. Then we made a connection. It's a wonderful feeling when your father becomes not a god but a man to you—when he comes down from the mountain and you see he's this man with weaknesses. And you love him as this whole being, not as a figurehead."

Robin was living in San Francisco at the time. His father had lived in Tiburon, where he had moved years before, when Robin was in high school. "So I was close. He'd had operations and chemotherapy. It's weird. Everyone always thinks of their dad as invincible, and in the end, here's this little, tiny creature, almost all bone. You have to say good-bye to him as this very frail being."

Robin had promised to scatter his father's ashes over the ocean in front of the house. "That day," Robin related, "we gathered right on the sea in front of where my parents live. It was funny. At one point I had poured the ashes out, and they're floating off into this mist, seagulls flying overhead. A truly serene moment.

"Then I looked into the urn and said to my brother, 'There's still some ashes left, Todd. What do I do?' He said, 'It's Dad—he's holding on.' I thought, 'Yeah, you're right, he's hanging on.' He was an amazing man who had the courage not to impose limitations upon his sons, to literally say, 'I see you have something you want to do— do it.' "

As his sadness over his father's death receded, Robin became aware of his new success. The Academy Awards were coming up. Could it be that Robin Williams might be nominated at long last?

He had already won a Golden Globe Award from the Hollywood Foreign Correspondents for his work on *Mork and Mindy*, but that was now eight years in the past. It was time for something bigger than that, something bigger than the Grammy he had won in 1979 for Best Comedy Recording, for *Reality . . . What a Concept!*

In due course the first award for *Good Morning, Vietnam* did come through—a Golden Globe. Since the Golden Globes frequently indicate who is going to win Academy Awards, excitement prevailed. Publicists worked overtime promoting Robin and his movie, and he found himself nominated for an Academy Award for Best Actor. The nomination itself put him a step ahead of where he had been in 1979, though it did not mean that he would win.

Robin was running against formidable competition. Jack Nicholson was up for an award for *Ironweed*; William Hurt was up for *Broadcast News*; Michael Douglas was up for *Wall Street*; and Marcello Mastroianni had been nominated for *Dark Eyes*. Also, there were other indications that the big award would go to someone other than the star of *Good Morning, Vietnam*. The picture had not been nominated for its script, for its director, or for best movie. And in the end it was Michael Douglas who won. (This was Douglas's second Oscar; he had already won as the producer of *One Flew Over the Cuckoo's Nest*.)

However, an unexpected gift came from the Emmy Awards; Robin won an Emmy for a benefit concert he had presented in England before Prince Charles and Princess Diana, *ABC Presents a Royal Gala*.

A Legendary Godot

By the time *Good Morning, Vietnam* was ready for screening, Robin Williams's private life had reached a new high. During the location shooting of the film, in Thailand, Marsha Garces had accompanied Robin as his secretary, adviser, and girlfriend.

What had started innocently enough had turned into a serious relationship. Marsha was Robin's soul mate during that long stint in Thailand making the picture that would be his breakthrough.

Pam Dawber, who had costarred with Robin on *Mork and Mindy*, had something to say about his relationship with Marsha Garces: "She's Robin's anchor. She's reality. Ground zero. She's very sane, and that's what he needs. She's incredibly loving too. And protective. She knows who is bad for him and who is good, and she helps keep the good relationships going."

Pam Dawber wasn't the only one who felt that way about Marsha Garces. Mark Johnson, the producer of *Good Morning, Vietnam*, said that "she was the hardest-working person on the set. She was there for him twenty-four hours a day. She truly loves him."

But at the same time, conflict persisted between Robin and his first wife, Valerie Velardi. Their problems had not been resolved by their separation agreement, and one destructive issue involved their son, Zachary.

Robin admitted this problem to *People* magazine. "What I'm trying to do now is to work with Valerie to transform our marriage into a relationship in which we share Zachary and do all we can to make him happy. I expect my involvement with Valerie to go on until I die."

Like most separation arrangements, Robin and Valerie's was difficult to abide by on the basis of a day-to-day and month-to-month working schedule. *People* quoted an observer: "She's not going to talk about it for publication, but Valerie's furious. What do you expect? Here's somebody who worked for her, and now Robin's living with her. Of course she's angry."

Valerie herself said nothing about her feelings toward Marsha Garces: "You're not going to get that out of me in a hundred years!"

During this interim, Robin felt that he was in a "gray area of life"—and living in such an area "is hard for everyone concerned. People have to get on with their lives."

Now that the long session in Thailand was over and Robin Williams was headed home, the question of his relationship with Valerie was once more coming to the fore.

He was asked if a reconciliation between him and Valerie was at all possible. He replied that such an idea had not really come up. On the other hand, when he was asked if there was any hint of divorce in the air, he said explicitly, "We haven't discussed divorce."

Valerie said exactly the same thing.

The question as to whether he might want to marry Marsha had apparently never been considered; or, if it had, nothing had been decided.

The main point, in Robin Williams's mind, was to protect Zachary from any harm in a possibly changing relationship.

"I watch Zachary absorbed in playing with his rockets, I listen to him whispering his multiple voices, and I think, 'That's where it comes from. That's the source.' "

Robin told another story about Zachary: "The teacher at his 'gestalt' day-care center was playing tapes of noises for the kids to identify. One was of a baby crying, and a little girl said, 'That's a *baby* crying.' Then they played a tape of laughter. 'I know! I know!' Zachary said. 'That's comedy!' And I thought, 'Riiiiight!' "

Regarding comedy from Zachary, Robin said: "I think sometimes he's been possessed by the spirit of a forty-five-year-old Jewish accountant, because I took him on vacation, he was walking down the stairs to a restaurant. He went, 'Look, the buffet looks very exciting. And after that I think I'll have some swordfish.' "

Is he a vegetarian, as his father had been? someone asked.

"No, no. He's Michelin. He's been raised on four-star restaurants. 'This salad is al dente.'"

"Right now," Robin said, "it's like living with a tiny Mormon. If you say something—say you're driving and somebody cuts you off—you go, you use that wonderful *f* word, and he says, 'Don't say that; they can't hear you.' 'Oh, I'm sorry, little Donny Osmond. Was that you eating a bug or am I crazy?'"

Robin's second marriage, when it occurred, was a surprise to almost everyone who knew the bride and the groom, and to the press, which was out of the loop. Obviously a divorce had been discussed and, in fact, finalized.

On Sunday, April 30, 1989, Robin Williams and Marsha Garces were married in a private ceremony at Lake Tahoe, California. A few close relatives and friends attended the wedding, including Robin's good friends Billy Crystal and Bob Goldthwait, both comedians. The newlyweds had given their guests only forty-eight hours' notice.

In Robin's words, "It was the SWAT-team school of weddings. We called everyone and said, 'Move it,' and they did move it. A good thing, too. The ceremony was very short, as was the guest list." He added, "It was one big show, like a telethon without an 800 number. It was a gas."

One interesting thing about this wedding was the fact

that Robin and Marsha had what they called a "development project" in the works: Marsha was pregnant, and the baby, by all accounts, was due to arrive in August 1989. And so the buzz continued. Robin could hardly contain himself.

When asked by Phil Donahue, "How's the marriage?" he couldn't refrain from ebullience: "Wonderful. Amazing. Amazing to be married, amazing to be expecting a child. To be expecting a child again is a wonderful thing. People think you have it together this time—you know, I had a son before. But is it any more—do you have it together?

"No, I'm still like—it's a wonderful combination of delight and terror at the same time. Knowing that you think that day—the day it happens, you know, the beeper goes off. I have to leave the set, I come home, 'Is everything okay?' And you walk in the door, like, 'I've got—get the car! The car, the car, the car! Gotta get the car, the car, the car, the car!' "

The baby actually arrived on July 30. She weighed nine pounds six ounces at birth, and the Williamses named her Zelda. Zachary Williams had a new half sister.

For the time being, at least, Robin Williams's hectic personal life had more or less settled down into a pleasant routine—in contrast to the many months and years it had been in an open field run from one disaster to another.

Robin had also achieved a peak in his professional life. There was now no question that *Good Morning, Vietnam* had been his breakthrough movie. He had made it at last, after many a false hope and many a flawed start. It was time for him to take a deep breath and perhaps relax a bit. It was time for him to think about where he had been, where he was at this moment, and where he would be going in the future.

The past was all laid out for him—all the mistakes and the one or two right moves he had made. From an analysis of the past, he should be able to limn out some kind of future path and get it right this time.

"I've always been looking for something with spirit. With a character who doesn't drive people crazy. In the past, I've had an odd habit of choosing projects that were the opposite of me, sometimes to my detriment. People are now saying about *Good Morning, Vietnam*, 'This film is basically you and what you do best. So why did you wait eight years?' "

Robin answered his own question. "Well, I made other choices. It was part ego, part stubbornness, in trying to do something unexpected. You're right. This is the first time I seem to be enjoying myself onscreen. . . . With *The World According to Garp* and *Moscow on the Hudson*, I was just trying for straight dramatic roles. I kept getting reviews like, 'It's a Maserati in neutral.' With *Good Morning, Vietnam*, I've tried to fuse the two. At least in America, it's got me back working again. This film offered a form of comedy I never had in any other film."

The right tone, the right slant, the right *spirit* had been a long time coming. Robin had exploded on the small screen with his first appearance as Mork. His hyperkinetic personality dominated television for a short time, but soon enough the role had burned out, perhaps because television used up too much of his energy and talent. He had no time to rest or relax or think things through.

Now, looking ahead, Robin saw a glimmer of light: the play *Waiting for Godot* by Samuel Beckett. And that definitely would not be a project Robin Williams could turn down. Mike Nichols staged it, casting Robin and Steve Martin as the two tramps Vladimir and Estragon. Putting Robin and Steve into this play was a calculated risk; but then, Bert Lahr, another well-known comedian, had been in the original production, starring with E. G. Marshall.

What Nichols wanted from Robin and Steve was their own clearly defined comic personalities: Martin's cheery oaf, gleefully mistaking every humiliation for genuine good fortune, and Williams's standup comic, the manic free-association improvisor, jumping from one crazy train of thought to another without stopping.

From the beginning of the project, there were dissenters. Die-hard Beckett fans—who would bring their own copies of the script to the theater—would shake their heads at the freedoms the two comedians would be taking with the dialogue.

However, it should be remembered that there was not one text of the play, but several different texts, representing revisions that Beckett had made over the years. How could anyone tell which was the real *Godot*? Indeed, Beckett was said to have given Mike Nichols carte blanche in interpreting the play.

Mike Nichols had originally wanted to set the action of *Godot* outside Las Vegas, but in the final stages of production he chose an unrelieved desert. That would replace the author's setting: "A country road. A tree." The desert was a generalization—which was what Beckett wanted in the first place.

The production was a hit with Kevin Kelly of the *Boston Globe*. The headline for his review was: "A Legendary *Godot*. Robin Williams and Steve Martin Shine in Beckett's Masterpiece."

Kelly cited a few departures from the script. For example, during the "quaquaquaqua" speech—when the supposedly mute Lucky breaks his silence in an unstoppable outburst—Robin Williams as Vladimir borrowed a program from someone seated in the first row and rapidly flipped through the ads. Steve Martin as Estragon pantomimed "Give me a break!" and then leaned over and, in a loud whisper, asked a patron in an aisle seat for the time. This was playing with Beckett's script, but Kelly liked it. He also liked the performances. He concluded his review with: "This is a *Godot* destined to become as legendary as the original production."

In all probability it will be legendary, but perhaps not for the right reasons. The opening night at Lincoln Center and the first few subsequent nights were sold out. However, not all the patrons were happy with the way Robin Williams and Mike Nichols treated the play.

The actors more or less shrugged off the negative reviews and the negative reactions during the play's run. Samuel Beckett's reaction, however, was another matter.

Beckett, then eighty-two, was in a hospital in Paris receiving care for his advanced arthritis. He wrote a scathing, no-holds-barred denunciation of their work. Beckett had not seen the production, but Jack Garfein, the producer-director, had sent him copies of the reviews and a copy of the program, and it was from these that he had formed his opinion. One of Beckett's milder statements was: "I deplore the liberties taken in N.Y. *Godot*, with text and onstage."

During rehearsals, Garfein had frequently mentioned that he was planning to do a film version of the play for television, with Williams and Martin. But now, with Beckett's disapproval casting a dark shadow, the film was probably a dead issue.

Robin Williams was hurt by Beckett's criticism. He attributed the negative reviews to the kind of audience Lincoln Center attracted: "They came because it was an event," he said, "the thing to do. We put our ass out and got kicked for it. Some nights I would improvise a bit and the hard-core Beckett fans got pissed off. We played it as a comedy team; it wasn't existential."

Williams was not his usual ebullient self in this phase of his theatrical career. He was unsettled because apparently he had somehow transgressed the bounds of good taste. And he was annoyed with himself for getting entangled in a situation that might not be easy to control.

Still, he has said several times that he enjoyed his run at Lincoln Center. He has also said that he would love to do another play—or possibly a reprise of *Godot*, but so far this has been just talk.

Robin sensed that he had been unfairly dealt with, although he could find no intellectual reason for feeling that way. His standups have never changed. He is the same legitimate actor he always was. But he has not appeared on the Broadway stage since that ill-fated run of *Waiting for Godot*.

"Wouldn't it be great to do *Godot* again?" he said in a recent interview. "Except this time I would be Lucky, the one who has the big long speech, the five-minute monologue. *Godot* . . . has great comic and tragic moments. It has everything you could ever want in a play. I would love to do that again."

Bankability

Once the box-office figures for *Good Morning, Vietnam* showed that Robin Williams had become a bankable commodity, he was under pressure to do the same kind of role again. In other words, the idea persisted in certain circles that another Adrian Cronauer would be an appropriate follow-up.

Yet at the same time, cooler heads were suggesting the opposite—something different, to prove that Robin Williams was a talented, many-faceted actor who could do almost anything.

He himself described the situation as an inner conflict: "It's a bit like, 'Get the laugh, go for the laugh, don't be afraid,' " he said, gesturing to suggest a little demon on his shoulder, "with an angel in rebuttal replying, 'No, just look at the camera. Look—don't say anything.' Then somehow you find it in between."

Ultimately, Robin realized that what he wanted more than anything else was to surprise audiences with his next role, and especially to wake up those who expected him to do the same thing as in *Good Morning, Vietnam*. Indeed, he had a history of varying his roles—one time a comic, for instance, and the next time a straight man.

The role he took on next was of an English teacher named John Keating, who bore no resemblance whatsoever to the more or less wild man he had played as Adrian Cronauer. Keating was an intellectual, a Rhodes scholar teaching at a posh private high school in Vermont.

"It's a different thing, and I like doing that," Robin said. "Sometimes I'll find one [role] is very dramatic and the other one is more tilted toward the manic and the comic."

In the film—*Dead Poets Society*—Keating is a new teacher at Welton Academy, a boys' prep school, circa 1959. Keating is an alumnus of Welton and is familiar with the curriculum and the attitude of the school's administration. Moreover, he knows how strict the rules are and how strictly they are enforced.

He brings with him his imagination and courage, and he promises himself that he will not stultify his students scholastically. He begins by encouraging all his students to seek out the unusual in the usual—especially in literature, but also in real life.

Before auditioning for this part, Robin had gone through a great deal of self-examination and had thought about his portrayal of this somewhat rebellious teacher.

Robin entertains the audience during a break in the show.

Robin Williams and costar Pam Dawber enjoy their success on the set of the hit TV show *Mork and Mindy.*

The many faces of Robin:
Whether playing a gay man
(playing a straight man), a
straight man playing a woman,
or a doctor playing a clown,
Robin Williams's movies were
huge box-office successes.

As Mrs. Doubtfire.

Dancing with Christine
Baranski in *The Birdcage*.

Robin gets a hands-on
experience at Mann's
Chinese Theatre while
wearing a rubber nose
from *Patch Adams*.

Robin's longtime friendship with actor Christopher Reeve began at the Juilliard School in New York. After Reeve's tragic accident, Robin remained a close friend and source of emotional support.

Robin yuks it up with Jack Nicholson at the seventieth annual Academy Awards. Robin won best-supporting Oscar for his role in the indie hit *Good Will Hunting*. Nicholson snagged best actor for his role as an obsessive curmudgeon in *As Good As It Gets*.

Robin and wife, Marsha Garces Williams.

That self-examination had involved Robin's knowledge of and instinct for standup comedy.

"It's like standup comedy," he said, "but this one has to be, rather than just a one-way street where it's going out, you have to keep a rapport. You have to kind of be attuned to where they're going and how far you can take them, and then pull back."

In discussing the role with Peter Weir, the director assigned to the picture, Robin brought the conversation around to his concern that moviegoers would expect to see Robin Williams "performing" again, performing like the manic he had played in *Good Morning, Vietnam*.

Weir and Williams felt that the tone of the picture should be set in the first scene, when Keating faces his class for the first time. There were two very different ways to film this scene: Keating could come into the room, jump up onto his desk, put on a phony accent, and startle the kids into laughing with him, binding them to him for the balance of the story; or he could simply walk through the door and look at the students in his class. It was the second version that they decided on: the muted approach.

"It sets the tone for the audience, too, that something different is going on. You've kind of gotten rid of that expectation of 'Here's the laugh riot.'"

And so the role turned out to be a fairly typical schoolteacher. "The only thing about this private school that differs from a public school is that in a public school sometimes people will heckle. You'll get, 'Yeah, right, yeah, sure. Baudelaire. I need that. I'm ready for that now.' " (The last is spoken by Robin in a punk's sarcastic voice.)

As the plot develops, Keating throws out the curriculum and tries to make his students think for themselves. He makes them tear out and toss away the introduction to their poetry text, since it explains how to measure the quality of verse "by the numbers" rather than by the emotion aroused in the reader.

In another instance, he marches them around on the campus like a drill sergeant to show them how easily a group of people can automatically fall into step without any thought or realization. He wants his students to break the habit of push-button behavior.

Seven of Keating's students take up his iconoclasm, and one of them learns that as a student at Welton, Keating had founded a sect called the Dead Poets Society. These seven revive the society, meeting secretly in a cave near the campus. They want to escape the staid, conformist 1950s, the Eisenhower years. Keating's brash nonconformity and his quips in class help some of the seven in their attempts to straighten out their lives.

The director, Peter Weir, an Australian, wanted to establish the proper mood among the actors playing the students. He told them that he was after the feeling of the "early Beatles," that they were portraying kids whose restless energy in 1959 would foreshadow the turbulent, perilous 1960s.

"I wanted to tap into that time frame where everything appears to be in its proper place, yet under the surface all these things are seething," Weir said. "Equally important as talent and appearance was their compatibility. I wanted everyone to feel that his contribution was critically important to the film—because it was."

To help these actors get into their roles, Weir would slip books of poetry under their doors at night: Rupert Brooke and Wilfred Owen (the English poets of World War I), Walt Whitman.

The film was shot on location at Saint Andrews School in Middletown, Delaware. It aroused considerable interest when it was released, and most of the critics liked it, though with reservations.

Mike Clark of *USA Today* wrote: "As enjoyable as it is, it's an oddball that doesn't fully connect. Hour 1 has all the laughs, including Williams . . . doing John Wayne as Macbeth. . . . Hour 2 switches to concentrate near-exclusively on a compelling power struggle between an acting hopeful . . . and his odious martinet-dad. . . ."

Pauline Kael of the *New Yorker* was struck with the way Robin Williams played John Keating: "Robin Williams's performance is more graceful than anything he's done before." But overall, she added, "*Dead Poets Society* is anomalous—a prestige picture."

When *Dead Poets Society* opened in 1989, two years after *Good Morning, Vietnam,* no one had any idea how it would strike the public. However, Robin Williams had taken good aim, and this one hit squarely on target. It established Williams as an actor of many talents, and it grossed $95.9 million in the American market alone, very close to the gross of *Good Morning, Vietnam* ($123.9 million). These remarkably different pictures, then, were equally successful.

Dead Poets Society does not seem to be a period piece, but it could not have been set anywhere else or at any time other than in the United States during the sedate postwar years. When people who lived through that period of suburban expansion describe it as the Eisenhower years, they do not mean to be laudatory. The school where John Keating teaches was typical of the period; one thinks of Holden Caulfield's escape from a very similar private school to spend his big evening in New York.

The difference is that in *Dead Poets Society* the maverick is Keating, the teacher, not the kids he is teaching. In effect, this film turns *Catcher in the Rye* inside-out, with the teacher as the dreamer and the rest of the school held captive.

Some of the byplay between Keating the unfettered dreamer and thinker and his conformist students may seem a bit hackneyed, but with the help of Robin Williams and Peter Weir the script and the outlook of the film avoid being maudlin or sentimental.

Actually, the original story had one element that would have ruined the picture: Keating was dying of leukemia, and his job at Welton was simply a return to the place where he had spent his happiest days. Weir and Robin decided to scrap that plotline, however, and without it the story became more sharply focused.

Robin Williams was the right actor for the role of John Keating. No one else could have established the teacher in the hostile eyes of a class of teenagers as Williams was able to do. His scholarly tricks of the trade were the right ones, and they caught the attention of the kids.

Dead Poets Society confirmed Williams's stature as an actor of talent and breadth.

The next film that Robin Williams made was *Cadillac Man*, in which he played a car salesman. This might seem to be yet another change of pace, but it really was not.

In *Good Morning, Vietnam*, the disk jockey's job was to charm and befriend hundreds of thousands of GIs he did not know—to make them his friends, to make them feel good, and, in the long run, to get loyalty, or something like loyalty, out of them.

In *Cadillac Man*, the job of the car salesman was to charm and beguile cynical, unfriendly, sarcastic customers—to make them love the cars in the showroom, to make them feel that these cars might make their lives better, and, in the long run, to extract loyalty from them—and perhaps a pocketful of cash.

The interesting thing is that in each case Robin Williams had selected a role that was tailored very closely to his own idea of what he did best—to befriend people and make them enamored of his charm and wit. His wit, of course, was a formidable element of his personality. This was what made him such an excellent standup comic; it was also a part of the fine actor that lurked deep within him, always there for the asking.

In each of these three films, Robin Williams utilized his most formidable talent to make a point. He was playing a standup comic in disguise, going through the routines of, first, a disk jockey; second, a schoolteacher; and third, a car salesman. Like a standup comic, he used his most powerful weapon to make those around him admire and follow him.

In a sense, *Cadillac Man* represented Robin Williams's toughest stance yet. Where can one find a more cynical, hypocritical, two-faced existence than in an automobile dealership, where even the toughest buyers usually meet their match? Here, Robin Williams was faced with the prospect of wooing would-be customers on the lot and at the same time trying to make everybody around him like him and believe in him. The fact that his own father had once worked in Detroit may have lent a bit of irony to the task he had set himself.

The story of *Cadillac Man* is relatively simple, although it is sometimes fraught with terror and hysteria. The director was Roger Donaldson. He was a New Zealand filmmaker, responsible for *No Way Out* (1987), a taut melodrama about a murder and a cover-up within the inner circles of the federal government; actually, it was a remake of *The Big Clock*, Kenneth Fearing's memorable novel. Donaldson had also made *Cocktail* (1988), with Tom Cruise, and *Smash Palace* (1981), a New Zealand film, which, coincidentally, also dealt with cars as symbols of sexual power.

The screenplay, by Ken Friedman, starts out with a bang. Robin Williams plays Joey O'Brien, formerly the star salesman at a luxury car dealership in Queens, New York. Now, his salesmanship has lost its edge because of his incessant womanizing. This womanizing includes one of his own ex-wives (Pamela Reed), the spoiled wife (Fran Drescher) of a Bronx businessman, and a sexy young fashion designer (Lori Petty).

Suddenly, a kook on a motorbike crashes through the dealership's plate-glass window, waving a machine gun in his hands. This nut, played by Tim Robbins, is Larry, who has flipped out and is searching for the man who slept with his wife.

Larry takes over the building, and everybody panics. It is up to Joey to make what he can out of this shambles. The core of the movie is the salesmanship that Joey applies, first calming down the hysterical Larry, then befriending him, and then pretending to conspire with him in an attempt to get the hostages out of harm's way.

Larry's wife, as it happens, is not one of Joey's conquests, though she is two-timing her husband with one of the other workers at the dealership.

What initially intrigued Robin Williams about this scenario was Joey's ability to take charge of the situation and neutralize Larry. In the end, Joey does indeed charm, cajole, and manipulate Larry, saving all the hostages and bringing the situation around to the capture of Larry.

"Why would I want to play some sleazy car salesman?" Robin Williams said to one writer. "Because the truth is they're not very different from standup comedians. Really." He went on, "There's the same rush when you know you've got your audience—you've made the sale. But there's the same element of possible failure, too, the same element of instantaneous readout when you know you're not doing well."

Joey is a nerd working his craft on a dangerous man— and in the process, saving the lives of a number of people, helping straighten out a marital tangle, and saving another man from jail. To bring realism to this role, Robin Williams did not depend solely on his father's work in Detroit. To absorb the feel of the car business, he also did some fieldwork: "I talked to a lot of dealers and salesmen, especially in New York, and they all told me the same thing. 'Be yourself, because you're selling yourself first.' "

Thinking about his foray into the car dealerships, Robin said, "Let's face it, most guys get their first car and have their first sexual experience about the same time, sixteen, and often simultaneously. That's probably why today's cars talk to you like a woman." He imitated a caressing whisper: "Come on in. The door is ajar. Check my oil. Don't be afraid. I'm ready."

Dave Kehr reviewed *Cadillac Man* in the *Chicago Tri-*

bune: "Near the end of *Cadillac Man*, Williams looks into the camera and exclaims, 'God, I love to sell!' It's the one line in the movie that really rings true. Williams is a salesman, and a darn good one; his only product is himself."

In *Movie and Video Guide 1994*, Leonard Maltin wrote: "Williams is terrific, as usual, playing an aggressive car salesman who may lose his job, his mistress, his other girlfriend, his Mafioso protector, and his daughter all during one eventful weekend."

Terrence Rafferty wrote in the *New Yorker:* "Robin Williams is in virtually every scene, and he's brilliant throughout." As for the picture, *"Cadillac Man* is shaggy and more than a little jittery itself."

Robin Williams chose *Cadillac Man* because he saw it as a tour de force that would let him be comic in a non-comic way. In this film, he had no shticks, and there were no routines in which he could show off his standup techniques.

The picture itself seemed promising when it was finally shot, and when it opened it looked good for the first few days. But quite soon, interest seemed to fall off. Other films like *Dick Tracy*, *Total Recall*, and *Die Hard 2* were attracting all the attention. In the end, *Cadillac Man* made only $27 million in the American market—not very good for a film that had been expected to make $100 million.

Redemption and Resurrection

Even with the heavy schedule of his motion picture work, Robin Williams continued to make appearances at comedy clubs throughout the country, to keep himself sharp. But the audience was not always as sharp as he was.

"I went out to perform last night here at the Holy City Zoo," he said. "The audience basically just looked at me. It was like being circumcised in the Grand Canyon. First five minutes, it was great, then I got political. [In a dum-dum voice:] 'Uh, well, I dunno, you know.' They shut down on me. I felt like William Buckley trying to interview Jesse Jackson. [Buckley drone] 'Ahhhh, Jesse Jackson, now that you're running with Reggie Jackson, let me ax you a question. . . .' "

After the realistic background of *Cadillac Man*, Williams decided to try something more whimsical and sentimental. He came up with a surrealistic fable about a homeless man's quest for the Holy Grail.

The title of this film was *The Fisher King*—the legendary fisher king being the guardian of the Holy Grail. In a literary sense, the story was an old-fashioned quest, in this case for redemption, as embodied by the grail.

Fables and fantasies do not always fare well on film, and *The Fisher King* was doomed from the beginning. It was written in a cryptic synonymous style, with each line of dialogue open to several sometimes contradictory interpretations.

On the surface, the story is realistic, since the search involves two homeless men. But essentially, even that surface reality is flawed. The man played by Robin Williams lives in an abandoned basement and so is not actually "homeless." But he is alienated from society, and throughout the story, this alienation is the most obvious thing about him and about the people he meets on his quest (played by Jeff Bridges, Amanda Plummer, and Mercedes Ruehl).

From his first days in New York City, Robin Williams had always been simultaneously fascinated and repelled by the scores of homeless people living on the streets. He had visited shelters and talked to the people there, and these talks had been fruitful, if not uplifting.

"You go and see people. You know it's not an image like they talked about later of the happy home. . . . You see that it's pretty painful stuff because the large majority in the major cities are former mental patients. You know they come from someplace and with some severe problems."

The character Robin plays is Parry, short for Parsifal. Parsifal is a figure in medieval romance; he is known as Percival in English mythology. The mythical Parsifal is a guileless fool who alone can heal the wound of Amfortas, the guardian of the Holy Grail, which is kept in its temple at Monsalvat (Mount Salvagge) in Spain. Eventually, Parsifal cures Amfortas and becomes in turn the guardian of the grail. Thus Parsifal—Parry—is the fisher king of lore.

Parry is a medieval scholar and was once a happily married man. Then his wife was murdered. He is unable, mentally, to withstand the trauma of his wife's murder, and her death has propelled him on a supernatural quest for redemption. The quest assumes medieval characteristics because of his deep immersion in the mythology of that era.

"The problem is that he created a whole other personality to deal with this horrible trauma," Robin explained. "I mean, Parry is not his name. It's a creation. It's a response. You can't deal with your past, so you create a whole other person based on Parsifal, who is a medieval fool."

In playing Parsifal, Williams reverted to type. The alienated schizophrenic, once a medieval scholar, became, in a way, the quintessential Robin Williams role. In effect, this film is an urban myth bordering on both genius and madness. It drew on Williams's qualities of innocence and gentleness to celebrate the undefinable dignity of the downtrodden.

As Parry veers over into medieval mythology, he needs

someone to act as his keeper and guide—and that need is filled by Jack, an ex–disk jockey, played by Jeff Bridges, who becomes Parry's soul mate. Jack is the voice of reason, confronting Parry's fantasy and make-believe.

When Mark McEwen at *CBS This Morning* interviewed Robin Williams, he asked what Williams wanted people to take away from this film, which seemed so obscure to so many viewers.

Robin tossed off a joke. "There's no Fisher King toys, I'm sorry about that. I think if they take away a sense of 'It's nice to have takeout in a movie, too.' Some compassion, yeah. My wife and I would like an order of compassion and just a side of innocence, and if you could throw in just a human connection, that would be great for the kids."

McEwen got the point. "Okay."

"I think it would be nice if they have just a look at the world slightly differently, a little like Dante's *Inferno*, a little bit like *Don Quixote*, and a bit like, you know, *Forty-Second Street*. It's got music."

"It's got everything." McEwan agreed.

Robin nodded. "It's got angst. It's got a little bit of hell. And that whole journey—that's why I can't give you one thing to say, 'This is what the movie's about.' It isn't one of those grand concept movies—it's a guy and his gun, it's a boy and his dog, it's . . . about simple compassion, about connecting with people."

The critics panned the film unmercifully, although several found it interesting. The reviewer for the *Los Angeles Times* said that Robin Williams's portrayal of the "cuddly schizophrenic Parry in *The Fisher King*" might be considered great by some East Coast critics, but Los Angeles didn't think much of it.

The critic at the *Chicago Tribune* was annoyed by "so much burly humanity, particularly of the overbearing Robin Williams variety."

The critic at the *Boston Globe* said: "You wish the film would go off the deep end, as Williams's character would do more often if it weren't so tied to his standup comic reflexes."

Robin Williams's interest in the homeless was not limited to his role in *The Fisher King*. It was something that had always been on his mind, and he wanted to do something about it. In spite of his busy acting career, he had been working on it mentally, if not vocally; and finally, in 1986, he acted.

He did not act alone. With him were two people who were equally dedicated: Billy Crystal (whom he knew through their shared interest in standup comedy) and Whoopi Goldberg. The three of them envisioned a show of some kind to raise money to help the homeless.

Robin and Billy were busy as usual with their many show dates, and that left the internal management more or less to Whoopi Goldberg, who was a genius at putting things together in a workable fashion.

She served as a center of the project, with Robin and Billy involved in bringing in the talent. The show developed into a real extravaganza.

It was called *Comic Relief*, and it immediately drew

dozens of seasoned pros. The attraction, of course, was the trio who had initiated the show. From the beginning, *Comic Relief* was a fantastic success. Within ten years the group had raised $35 million, all of which was distributed to a number of relief efforts.

Whoopi Goldberg told *Playboy* in January 1997: "The boys have sort of nurtured me along, and now, I've finally come into my own with them. They're a tough duo. They are so fast. It took me until three or four years ago to just bust in. They were always really good to me, encouraging me, doing Pow! You're on! I always considered myself the Vanna White of *Comic Relief*, because I do all the serious stuff—the information, the phone numbers. I finally busted loose with them. Now we run wild."

Robin Williams's film schedule precluded his attendance at many other functions, but he always found the time and energy to do another bit for *Comic Relief*.

One routine had Robin and Billy Crystal acting together, with Crystal in front of Robin. Robin thrust his fist through Crystal's legs, making it look as if Crystal were sporting a large and ugly erection.

The programs continued through the 1980s and 1990s, raising millions of dollars each year:

Comic Relief I (1986)	$2.5 million
Comic Relief II (1987)	$2.5 million
Comic Relief III (1989)	$5 million
Comic Relief IV (1990)	$7 million

Comic Relief V (1992)	$6.7 million
Comic Relief VI (1994)	$7.8 million
Comic Relief VII (1995)	$5 million

Of all the performers, Robin Williams has become best known for raising money for the homeless.

At this point, Robin Williams began to experience déjà vu with regard to his acting career. He could have become a victim of one of his own word-association time warps, for time did seem to bend back on itself. He met again one of the people he had briefly encountered on his way up.

Penny Marshall, Garry Marshall's sister, had been one of Robin Williams's main supporters even before *Mork and Mindy*. In fact, she had been instrumental in helping Robin get the role of the alien from outer space on *Happy Days*— the role that led to *Mork and Mindy* as a spin-off.

Now Penny was a director working with superstars in some movies that had done well at the box office and in the eyes of the critics: Whoopi Goldberg in *Jumping Jack Flash*, Tom Hanks in *Big*, and others. She was looking around for another film, and she happened upon a script adapted from a book by Dr. Oliver Sacks, *Awakenings*.

The book fascinated her, and she immediately sought out people who might back the picture. Here's a brief account of what Sacks, a neurologist, did.

In 1969, Sacks joined the psychiatric staff at Bainbridge Hospital in the Bronx. He immediately became interested in a group of patients who had been victims of an encephalitis epidemic in the 1920s that had left them immobilized. They were now little more than frozen statues, unable to speak or act. Among them was a once brilliant student named Leonard Lowe, now locked into a silent, frozen world.

When a new drug called L-dopa came on the market for victims of Parkinson's disease—whose symptoms are similar to those of the encephalitis victims—Sacks got permission (given reluctantly, however) to try it out on the group at Bainbridge. In what appeared to be a miracle, the drug wakened them all, one by one, and a new life began for these long-forgotten victims. But side effects soon appeared, with disastrous results that made their lives even grimmer than before.

In a nutshell, this was the story that intrigued Penny Marshall. It had also intrigued Harold Pinter, the British playwright, who had written a play titled *A Kind of Alaska* about this "awakening." The people at Fox were interested in the script, too, though they could not get a go-ahead from the top brass. Now Penny began searching for actors, and she snared Robert De Niro, who had almost signed on for *Big*, her earlier hit. When she persuaded him to play the patient Leonard Lowe, she knew she was halfway home.

She had been impressed by Robin Williams's acting in *Dead Poets Society*, and she asked De Niro to see it and then confer with her. He agreed with her about Robin

Williams, and they decided to enlist him in the production, playing Sacks. Robin said this about the script:

"I sobbed. I happened to read it on a plane, probably from San Francisco to Los Angeles, and I was quite moved—to the point where a stewardess thought something was wrong. It devastated me, you know?"

The picture was shot in an institution in Brooklyn. There were patients on the lower floors, so the movie crew was limited to the top floor. Oliver Sacks was hired as a technical adviser. He appeared often on the set and gave as much advice as he thought necessary.

Robin Williams was surprised at the conflicts within Sacks—not psychological but physical conflicts.

"To play him was an amazing combination of things. He's Schweitzer and Schwarzenegger, a gentle man who used to squat-press six hundred pounds. He's incredibly shy, but aggressive in how he pursues an idea."

Robin plunged into the routine, studying his model carefully, trying to imagine Sack's mind-set and probe his inner feelings.

"I was playing him full out, complete with the accent and mannerisms," Williams said. And this alerted Penny to the fact that a problem was being created by the way Robin was approaching the role.

She drew him aside, and they talked. First of all, she told him to drop some of the behavior he was copying literally and to put more of himself into the character.

Robin pointed out that it was difficult to uncopy the

man he had come to copy, because Sacks was physically present every day on the set. It was hard to play him and not play him at the same moment.

Sacks himself had noticed that Robin was imitating him: "I was a little scared when I learned that someone with such powers of apprehension as Robin was getting me as a subject, because he does have this extraordinary, at times involuntary, power of mimicry. It was like a twin, like encountering someone with the same impulses as one's own."

Finally, Penny had an idea. It was just a psychological trick: she suggested that they change the name of the doctor; "Oliver Sacks" would become "Malcolm Sayer" in the movie. At first not everyone was enthusiastic about this change, but in the long run, it worked.

"It freed both him and me simultaneously," Robin said, "because Oliver had been coming to the set all the time to help us, and for him it was like walking into a three-dimensional mirror."

Robert De Niro insisted on acting his scenes in chronological order—not in the usual mixed-up fashion decreed by a script and a director. Although Penny Marshall knew this would be a tougher schedule to maintain, she agreed. De Niro had a reason.

Robin had never worked with De Niro. And because of the exigencies of the role, the two had no dialogue together for quite a while. De Niro, as Lowe, was a rock, a stone face, a statue. That was all. Then came the day that Lowe "awakened."

Robin had this to say about shooting that scene: "That was the most amazing day. For the first couple of weeks, he was, you know, a rock. The only thing different from take to take would be if he blinked, where his eyes were looking. And the first time he spoke, it flattened me. I guess I realized he did all that other stuff to work up to this moment. It was truly powerful."

De Niro put it this way: "I wanted just to be careful about the moment and not kind of break a certain magic, or whatever you want to call it, in terms of the awakening."

Penny Marshall was amused at Robin's reaction to the full power of De Niro's acting. "Bobby had basically been staring," she said. "Then that night, for the first time, Bobby acts. So Robin goes, 'Oh, . . . he checks in. I see he's going to act now.' He got a little nervous. I said, 'You're fine, you're okay.' He just hadn't seen him act before. Yeah. He knocks you right out of your seat."

During the filming of an action scene in which Robin was trying to restrain De Niro, there was a sudden loud crack and it was obvious that someone was hurt.

"We heard a crack," De Niro said. "You could hear it on the sound track in the rushes."

Robin knew what it was. "I went, 'Oh, no!' And they thought, 'God, that's great acting,' because I was going, 'Oh, my God, oh Jesus, oh God—' "

Indeed, Penny Marshall was wondering why Robin was overacting: "Robbo—tone it down a little bit."

De Niro went on with the scene. When he moved over

to a window, as part of the action, Penny could see what was wrong.

"Only when we yelled 'Cut!' and I could get around to the other side could I see the blood coming from Bobby's nose. We did nine more takes, because Bobby said, 'No, let's keep going.' His doctor wasn't in his office yet, so he said, 'All right, I can't do anything now, let's just keep going.' He knew the next day it would be worse and he would get black eyes, so we just shot."

De Niro later said: "Oh, I was annoyed, but it was just one of those freak accidents. . . . It started swelling up and I got black and blue, and it changed the size of my face, so I had to stop shooting for about a week."

Robin Williams shrugged. "It was in various press accounts that I got angry and broke his nose. If that was true, I don't think I'd be here today, going, 'Let's talk.' I mean, not with my own teeth."

De Niro (laughing): "The thing is, my nose was broken once before, and he knocked it back in the other direction—straightened it out. It looks better than it did before."

"His assistant said he should send me a check for reconstructive surgery," Robin observed.

The critics were unanimous in praising the general message of the picture. Jay Carr of the *Boston Globe* wrote: "*Awakenings* is the kind of film that could easily self-destruct in a pall of uplift. What saves it dramatically—although at heartbreaking cost to the patients—is that after the seeming miracle of L-dopa, there's trouble."

Pauline Kael of the *New Yorker* saw the film's inner tensions and contradictions as the result of an underlying conflict between Penny Marshall and Oliver Sacks, who had lived the part of Sayer and written the book on which the script was based. Kael said that Marshall "exalts the normal, and she keeps zapping us to feel the humanistic, the obvious. (Her forte is to make blandness ring true.)" Thus the original story was made more sentimental.

As was his habit, Robin Williams had chosen a character quite different from the one he had just finished playing—the fisher king. Williams knew what Sacks, or Sayer, was really like under all his bear hugs and what might be considered his bedside manner.

After the initial scenes, in which Robin had copied Sacks's physical mannerisms, he managed to make Sayer more scientific and more professional.

Robin also submerged all his own impulses, more or less stifling his tendency to burst forth and clown around. He truly became an absentminded professor and played the role of a quiet, soft-spoken, thoughtful man with deep personal interest in the patients he dealt with every hour of the day.

So the role became another new departure for Robin. It was also the perfect counterfoil for the role De Niro was playing.

By adopting this low-key approach, Robin was putting himself on the sidelines and playing a character without much volatility, without any slam-bang emotions, without the dramatic heights and depths of the "awakener," Lowe.

And that made the role far more powerful: Sayer was a truly sweet, friendly, thoughtful man trying to cope with his patients' eccentricities and idiosyncracies.

Robin was complimented not only by the critics but also by his fans for the role he played opposite the impulsive, explosive De Niro. And although by its very nature the film was not slated to be a top-notch moneymaker, it grossed a strong $52 million in the American market.

As for Robin's future work, he began to crave a little more action and excitement in his next movie role—and perhaps just a bit more theatricality.

Some Hits, Some Flops (1)

Chapter Twelve

Good Morning, Vietnam was such a box-office bonanza that in Hollywood and the other film centers of the world, Robin Williams was considered a powerhouse. But it was *Dead Poets Society* that made the public—and those in the entertainment industry—see him as more than just a talent in the standup comedy division; this picture established him as a serious actor.

Dead Poets Society brought in a substantial $94.6 million domestically, and $140 million in Europe. It also became a tremendous hit in other parts of the world.

In Japan, for example, it moved audiences so much that theater lights were kept low for at least five minutes at the end of each showing in order to allow the viewers time to compose themselves before going home. One reason for this reaction was that the Japanese school system is as rigid as Welton Academy in the film.

Robin was still a hit where he had always been a hit—in comedy—and also a hit as a dramatic actor. At the same time, his personal life was becoming more stabilized. In the last days of 1991, his wife, Marsha, gave birth to her second child (Robin's third). It was a boy whom they named Cody.

"I've always wanted to have somebody from the rodeo in the family," Robin told Oprah Winfrey once. In imitation of a rodeo announcer: "Coming out of the chute, Number One!" Then, kidding in his usual vein: "Playing with that umbilical like a lariat. Never met a man he didn't like, but—'Hell! I've been inside for a long time!'"

Robin did standup comedy on television shows while he was plugging his films. It was a busy life, but he had settled down and he was sticking to a much healthier routine.

After *The Fisher King* and *Awakenings* there were several good pictures—some better than others, but all quite successful. *Hook* was followed by *Toys*, *Being Human*, and *Aladdin*. *Aladdin* featured Robin Williams only as the voice of the genie.

Of all these pictures, probably the least impressive in terms of money was *Hook*. Disney had hoped that it would gross at least $250 million, but it made only $117 million.

Hook is a send-up, part fact and part fantasy, in which Robin plays a yuppie seeking redemption from the fictional villain Captain Hook. The yuppie himself is a grown-up Peter Pan, now called Peter Banning. The plot is convoluted.

Peter Pan grows up and moves to America, the land of opportunity, where he feels he will have a better life than in old, tradition-bound Great Britain. He becomes a successful attorney and turns into a workaholic who has completely forgotten his youth as Peter Pan. The story opens when he takes his family to England on a visit.

There, his children are kidnapped by the villain from his past, the pirate captain who tormented Peter in Never-Never Land. Hook is bored with being a villain in somebody else's past and wants to reassert himself—hence the kidnapping. And so Peter Banning sets out to find his children, battle his pirate nemesis, and do in Captain Hook for good.

The initial idea was Steven Spielberg's, and with Spielberg running the show, Robin felt he had nothing to worry about at the box office. The man who had made *Jaws*, *E.T.*, and *Close Encounters of the Third Kind* could hardly fail with a sequel to *Peter Pan*.

Yet there were certain similarities between *Hook* and *Popeye*, Robin's first major film, which had been a disaster even though it was made by Robert Altman. "This is a little frightening," Robin said. "That's why doing Peter Pan is still a little like, ooohhh, another character with the name P. Another icon. Oh, man. You want that pressure?" He added, "It's hard because people want to know you're a certain thing. They still say, 'That's the little manic guy. He's the little adrenaline guy. Oh, yeah, he touches himself. He doesn't do that anymore. But wait a minute. He's the little manic guy who played the really quiet guy and then the really scary guy. Oh, no, wait. . . .' "

Christopher Reeve had a theory about Robin's outlook: "He's treating the whole film-star experience as though he were still a student, with an appetite for new experiences, instead of being guarded and cautious and safe."

For Robin, plunging himself into the role of the young Peter Pan was not easy. As he put it, he had to shed "twenty-five pounds, a conscience, all your business agendas—get rid of those real quick, lose every memory after the age of fourteen and try and go back to the age of ten."

He admitted that there had been a time when he did not want to face up to certain things—when, in effect, he did not want to grow up. "There was a time when I didn't want to deal with things. I was performing, playing, never wanting to stop and examine anything—especially relationships. I just wanted to keep moving. If you keep moving, they'll never find out who you are. Then you realize: 'What are you doing?' "

At one point a therapist told Robin: "The best therapy for you is just play with your kid, and I think you'll find that quite fulfilling."

Robin thought, "He was right."

Also, at times Robin knew that by being a comedian, he was preventing people of consequence from taking him seriously.

"It was a question of if you could contain it sometimes. All that energy that would go into finding the right line, create a person, create a character that people would follow rather than have to always look for the line—the funny line."

Hook was by no means easy to make. It was rumored to have cost $80 million, and when it was cut, its final running time was 144 minutes. Shooting took six months, with Robin Williams suffering the most from the constant on-camera work; he was in almost every scene.

At this point, Robin was forty, and he was playing a youthful Peter Pan. How could he manage it? There was, first of all, the problem of his body hair. He had often joked about the enormous amount of fur on his body. While he was playing in *Hook*, he had to shave his arms and upper body completely every other day.

Another problem was trying to convey an upbeat attitude in his posture and his actions. He could see why most of the people who played Peter Pan had been women. Getting the wrong body posture or speaking the words too heavily would ruin everything, and this is what he had been worried about since the inception of the project. Would *Hook* be another *Popeye*?

Bob Hoskins, the British actor who played Hook's first mate, Smee, took Robin aside one day and gave him a piece of advice that Robin eagerly accepted. Hoskins suggested that Robin play Peter Pan as if he were slightly insane.

It worked. At least, Robin felt better about the delivery of his lines. The grueling experience was something he would never forget, however.

Terrence Rafferty, who had just replaced Pauline Kael

as the *New Yorker*'s film critic, called *Hook* "a blockbuster fiasco." This was close to the truth, although a fiasco is an incontrovertible error, while *Hook* did have good points as well as bad.

Hook opened (unusually) on a weekday—Wednesday, December 11, 1991—with a special preview the previous evening. On that Tuesday night and Wednesday, it took in over $2 million. Everybody breathed a sigh of relief; cost overruns had plagued the film, but now the payoff seemed to be in sight. By the following Monday, however, *Hook* had taken in only $14.2 million from its opening weekend and $17.7 million for its first six days. Basically, the problem was its length: it ran 144 minutes. The viewers were not tired, but it was physically impossible to run *Hook* as many times as a shorter film.

The TriStar execs were apt to be touchy with regard to money, and they were dubious about the final figures for *Hook*. Also, in spite of Rafferty's blast in the *New Yorker*, other reviews came through with nice tributes to Robin Williams and Dustin Hoffman. But there was a sense of something amiss, even among *Hook*'s supporters, because the story of Peter Pan was lighthearted, spirited, and youthful while *Hook* was somber and realistic. The lightness and the heaviness just didn't mix, resulting in a film that didn't seem to click with either adult or child audiences.

In the end, though, *Hook* turned out to have unexpectedly strong "legs," making a whopping $300 million worldwide. It also was a huge hit as a home video, selling millions of units worldwide.

As for Robin Williams, he came through unscathed. Even the flying he had to do (à la Mary Martin in the original *Peter Pan*) left him uninjured. His scenes with Dustin Hoffman, in which Peter tried to shout down the oppressive, fearsome Captain Hook, all came off nicely, with the two pros enjoying themselves, and added drama and suspense to the film as a whole.

What was next for Robin Williams?

Toys is basically a fable to illustrate a point of view about warfare and human suffering. On the surface, it is a struggle by family members to control the destiny of Zevo Toys.

Just before his death, the owner, Kenneth Zevo, wills the company to his brother Leland (Michael Gambon), a frustrated former army general. Leland swears that he is going to bring some efficiency and discipline to the haphazardly run company.

Set against Leland is Leslie Zevo, played by Robin Williams, and his sister Alsatia, played by Joan Cusack. (Leslie and Alsatia are Leland's nephew and niece.) These two live on the borders of fantasy, having spent their lives inventing windup toys to amuse children, and they are victims of their fantasy world. They have none of Leland's muscularity or willpower.

Analyzing his own role, Robin said: "He's very serious about his playing, because it's his life, it's his work, and it's also his world. He doesn't know an awful lot of anything else. He's a little bit of an emotional savant that way; that's why he has to use a puppet to meet people.''

Once the ex-general has taken over the company, he tries to create a War Toys Division, which the Zevo clan has traditionally forbidden. He is frustrated in that attempt, but then he starts a secret project to develop cheap, miniature weapons that can be operated electronically by kids mesmerized by video games.

Leslie knows he must stop this at all costs, and that is the crux of the story. The climax is a battle between HO-scale tanks and traditional windup toys that underlines the message of the film.

The most attractive thing about *Toys* was that Barry Levinson was going to direct it; the story had been in his mind for years. Levinson had been responsible for *Good Morning, Vietnam*, so Robin wanted to be involved.

Levinson also wanted Robin to do *Toys*. ''Robin was always at the top of the list,'' he said, ''even at the beginning. I just felt he had the right sensibilities for it. He has an innocence in him—that man-child thing—and that is really the heart of the movie.''

''Barry told me I was the only actor who would look natural playing with toys,'' Robin said. ''I had to really think that over for a moment, that remark about my playing with toys, but I took it as a compliment. So why do I say yes to this? Basically, I did it because of Barry. He described this world to me and I said, 'That's wonderful. I'd like to take that ride with you.' ''

Barry Levinson knew exactly what he was getting into. He has always said that he prefers to work that way. "That's the fun of it. There's nothing more fun than to know that you've got the thing on the page, and if anything new comes up, that's great. I really do like to work that way, with Robin and with other actors, too. The difference is that Robin can give me maybe fifteen different choices, where some other actor might just come up with a couple. That's his genius."

In a way, most directors knew that Robin was as much a writer as an actor—that is, he was usually given some leeway in rewriting a script if it needed rewriting. But he never got writing credits, nor did he want them.

Robin and Barry Levinson discussed the story of *Toys* many times. "Barry talks about toys as still being a symbol of innocence to children," Robin said. "Regular toys: not the triple Rambo impersonator dolls. There's still something about the 'toy' toys that people think is very special. That's why the battle at the end of the film is too much for some people."

To play the role of Leslie Zevo in *Toys*, Robin Williams dyed his hair blond. "I wanted him to look like a Ken doll gone berserk. He has a troubled personality. He's really one of my favorite characters and one of the saddest. He can't relate to people without toys.

"I was an only child, and it was lonely. So I developed a lively imagination. Leslie is an only child in a way, having a sister who's exceedingly eccentric. I could relate to him on a lot of levels."

Robin had faith in the picture, but reviewers felt differently when the movie was released.

Jay Carr's review for the *Boston Globe* was typical: "It plays like something that's been left in the incubator too long. It's not only the flattest film in which Williams has appeared, it's also the most anemic Levinson has directed."

Toys was released in 1992, during the lucrative Christmas season. The marketing strategy was typical of Hollywood: "The story's about toys! We'll get every kid in the world to see the picture!"

Actually, nothing could have saved *Toys*—from the beginning, the picture did not know what it was, and neither did the viewers. Some saw it as a black comedy, "Dr. Strangelove Meets FAO Schwarz." Some saw it as a straight comedy, with pratfalls, slapstick turns, and comic riffs. Some saw it as a fantasy.

It opened disastrously. The critics didn't know what to make of it. Kids didn't know what to make of it, though it was supposed to be "their thing." Parents were bored with it.

The box office was even worse; it started down and continued down. In all, *Toys* earned only $23.3 million in American revenues; this was the worst showing for a Robin Williams picture since before *Good Morning, Vietnam*.

Toys was an anomaly: a failure by Barry Levinson. Actually, no one had thought it through. Levinson had originated the script and brought it with him when he joined

Fox in 1978. It was to be his first picture for Fox. But there were management changes, and the script lay on the shelf for fourteen years. The new management considered it unfunny, and it languished.

After the film's inauspicious debut, the studio pulled it and simply let it finish out its run instead of spending money to publicize it.

Robin himself blamed no one for the movie's failure. In fact, he is rather philosophical about it. He once said that when his children want to express doubt about something he is telling them, they sometimes wink at one another and say, "He made *Toys*."

Some Hits, Some Flops (2)

Chapter Thirteen

Being Human wasn't exactly a run-of-the-mill picture. It was, in effect, a tour de force for Robin Williams. But then, which of Robin's pictures was not a tour de force in some way? Let's say *Being Human* was a gimmick—a picture composed of five separate stories rather than just one, all five dealing with a man named Hector, played by Robin Williams.

Each of these stories was totally unrelated to the others except for the fact that Hector appeared in them all: first as a Neolithic caveman, second as a Roman slave, third as a poor traveler in the Middle Ages, fourth as a servant to a New World explorer, and fifth as a stressed-out property manager with a dubious past in New York City.

This strange picture was the brainstorm of the British director Bill Forsyth, who had done the well-received *Local Hero* (1983) and *Gregory's Girl* (1981). *Leonard Maltin's Movie and Video Guide 1994* called *Local Hero* "a little gem'' and *Gregory's Girl* "enjoyable, if perhaps a bit over-rated.''

"I've just finished *Being Human*,'' Robin Williams joked at one interview when he was on tour to plug the opening of the film. "Boy, that sounds like a sad thing to do. But really, it's a very interesting film. It's very weird. An intimate epic. Making it taught me a kind of evolutionary humility—it gives you a real sense of who you are, where you came from, what we are as an animal. Emotionally, we really haven't evolved so much in six thousand years.''

About making the picture, Robin recalled, "It was also a brutally hard shoot. Being in Scotland, running around in cold weather. You realize why your testicles were designed to go up. Insulation.''

The best sequence in *Being Human* is probably the first—the caveman and his tribe. This one is frenetically Robin Williams. Language, at least the kind familiar to us, has not yet been invented, and Hector and his family communicate with one another in strange grunts, giggles, and hand signs. All are dressed in animal skins.

They live idyllically in Britain until a crew of foreigners come from across the sea and kidnap Hector's wife and kids. These interlopers speak a foreign language, and the cave people can't even express their displeasure but are forced to submit with dumbstruck idiocy.

In the second segment, Robin plays a house slave to a Roman merchant (John Turturro). The merchant has disgraced himself by bungling some kind of business deal and has decided that, to atone, he must open his veins. He wants his slave to commit suicide along with him, to show how much he loves his master. But the wily slave finally manages to elude this fate and find solace with a beautiful slave girl.

In the medieval segment, Hector, returning from a trip, meets a flirtatious widow (Anna Galiena) and a somewhat hypocritical priest (Vincent D'Onofrio) who is also attracted by the widow.

Hector next appears in the New World as the servant of a Portuguese explorer (Hector Elizondo) who has been shipwrecked on an island. The explorer must decide the fate of some crewmen accused of drinking all the water; the hanging scene, shown in backdrops, turns out to be comic.

In modern New York City, Hector is a divorced building manager who is trying to get reacquainted with his kids at a beach house. Lorraine Bracco plays his girlfriend. This modern sequence was filmed at Stinson Beach in gorgeous color.

A review by Marylynn Uricchio in the *Pittsburgh Post-Gazette* reads in part: "It's Williams's movie from beginning to end, and easy to see why he would jump at the chance to play so many demanding roles."

There has always been an imp of comedy within Robin Williams, which seems ready to leap out whenever it is called on. During this busy period of filmmaking, the imp appeared again, when Robin learned that Disney was making an animated feature of *Aladdin*. The part of the genie interested Robin.

He agreed to do this role for only $75,000, though at that time he could command anywhere from $4 million to $8 million a picture. He did the genie for scale because he wanted the role.

"I went into a room and started improvising," Robin said, "and these guys kept throwing ideas at me. It just got wild. They let me play. That's why I loved it—it was like carte blanche to go nuts. Of course, there were times when I'd go tasteless, when I knew 'the mouse' was not going to approve. 'Oh, come on, boy. Rub the lamp, the big spout. Don't be afraid!' "

There was so much improvisation that the filmmakers had to make their drawings in response to Robin's rapid-fire ideas instead of following the usual procedure: pictures and animation first, then the looping of the voice.

"It was a liberating experience. It's very freeing to know that what I say, they will draw. It's like Field of Cartoons: 'If I say it, they will draw.' And they drew almost anything I said."

Robin Williams received no special billing for his work in *Aladdin*, although he said that his name appeared somewhere along with the millions of others involved in the film.

"Everyone knew I was doing the genie. I just wanted it to be a supporting role. The film would have been a big hit under any circumstances. They tell me I kicked it into overdrive, and I'm glad for its success."

"Into overdrive" hardly conveys what happened at the box office. *Aladdin* was released in November 1992 and was a blockbuster hit from the start. In the next weeks the lines of moviegoers grew longer and longer.

Aladdin earned $217.4 million in the American market, but that was only part of the story. The video market was also a gold mine; everybody who had seen the picture apparently wanted a copy at home. During the first four weeks after the video was released, Disney sold 15 million copies in the United States alone.

According to Disney's projections, the picture may have made almost $750 million—and Robin Williams had done his role for scale!

There were ancillary benefits for Disney, but there was also evidence of some bad blood between Robin and the Mouse.

When the picture was released, a number of Disney toys connected with it were also put on sale. During the flurry of marketing them, the name of Robin Williams became prominent in the ads on television.

At that point Robin put his foot down. "It was a violation of an agreement that we made. I said, 'Listen, I'll do the cartoon, and I'll do it for scale. I don't care. Just don't use my voice to sell merchandise.' "

Although the rift between Robin and Disney lasted for some time, it turned out to have been nothing more than a simple misunderstanding. Disney had used an actor pretending to be Robin Williams as the genie, not Robin's own voice.

While Williams and Disney were in contention over this issue, the studio made a sequel to *Aladdin* called *The Return of Jafar*. *Jafar* was intended to go straight to video and would not be released as a film in theaters. The experiment was wildly successful. Over 10 million units sold rapidly, making *Jafar* one of the twenty top-selling videos of all time. But this time Robin Williams was not the voice of the genie. Dan Castellaneta (who played Homer Simpson in the Fox network's sitcom) had filled in because Robin was on the outs with the Disney brass.

Later, after a change in management, Robin and the studio heads finally reached an amicable agreement prohibiting the studio from using Robin's voice to sell merchandise tied to *Aladdin*. In 1996, Disney hired Robin once again to be the voice of the genie for the second sequel to *Aladdin: Aladdin and the King of Thieves*.

"Some people have actually said the genie is my best work," Robin told one film critic. "Thanks very much, but . . . hmmm. I don't know if that's a compliment."

The year after the original *Aladdin*, during the Christmas season of 1993, Robin was the narrator of the holiday perennial *Peter and the Wolf*, with the San Francisco Youth Orchestra in Davies Hall in San Francisco. The show was an admirable success.

There was also television work at this time, although

Robin thought he'd had enough of network television and particularly of acting in a series. He agreed to appear in four episodes of *Homicide: Life on the Streets*, to be aired in January 1994. His role was the husband of a woman killed in a street robbery.

Williams liked this role because it was so different from what he had been playing in films and in his own specials on television. Also, it was Williams's colleague Barry Levinson who had created *Homicide*, and Robin owed him something.

In these four episodes, Williams plays a tourist in Baltimore, where the show is set. His wife is murdered by street thugs, in full view of their two children. Williams's role called for him to express his grief, of course, and he was featured in confrontation with the show's regular characters, hard-bitten cops whose compassion has long since been crushed under the weight of urban indifference.

The script gives Robin cause to turn against these men who are really trying to help him. Daniel Baldwin, for example, chuckles over the fact that he'll draw overtime pay because the mayor's office is demanding quick arrests to assuage the tourist lobby. And when Robin proves unable to describe the street kids clearly, Richard Belzer (as Officer Munch) becomes sarcastic and contemptuous. This causes Robin to blow his top. He then lodges a bitter complaint with the lieutenant (Yaphet Kotto). Instead of satisfaction, the superintendent gives him a short lecture on urban crime.

The fourth episode ends when the killers are caught, tried, convicted, and sentenced. Williams is present at the trial and watches everything with a jaundiced eye. He thought the trial would be the final chapter, or perhaps that it would seal the tragedy in a package that he could keep forever in some other part of his mind. But he gets no help from it; he gets only the cold hard facts.

Homicide had been sinking in the Nielsen ratings, but these four episodes helped somewhat. The show was still being broadcast in 1999, although with major changes in its original cast.

Robin Williams's guest appearances undoubtedly led some viewers to tune in, and evidently many stayed to watch what happened afterward. It can't be stressed too much that his acting was perfect for the role and the audience.

Alias Robin Williams

I n 1993, Robin Williams and his wife, Marsha, formed a production company, which they called Blue Wolf Productions. She was named a producer and president of the fledgling company. There was a specific reason that the company was formed. Marsha Williams explained it in detail to a reporter:

"I wanted to have control over when and where we were going to shoot. More than anything else, the company was formed in order to protect Robin."

The meaning of the name "Blue Wolf" was obvious: "It's Robin, because he's the blue wolf."

Robin Williams cut in: "The blue-eyed wolf. Actually, it's just because we love wolves."

"And they're on our wedding rings," Marsha added.

Robin, with a grin: "And I'm hairy."

Marsha had been Robin's assistant for several years during the shooting of his various films, and she had accompanied him to Asia for *Good Morning, Vietnam*. She had been credited as his assistant on the final cut of *Toys*, but "assistant" can be a fuzzy word. An assistant might simply run out for coffee, but Marsha Williams was always looking for material that Robin might perform, especially in film ventures—hence the new title "producer."

Marsha had always been an insatiable reader, and she spent much of her time going over material that might work for Robin Williams as an actor. She read all sorts of things. Robin was in the habit of reading "all sorts of things," too, including comic books and esoteric publications. But it was Marsha who read a children's book by an Englishwoman named Anne Fine, titled *Alias Madame Doubtfire*, soon after its publication in 1987 in Britain. Marsha was impressed, though nothing came of her interest at the time.

Meanwhile, a producer named Matthew Rushton and the late Frank Levy picked up the book, and it eventually wound up at Twentieth Century–Fox, where it was assigned to a writer for a script. The scriptwriter was Randi Mayem Singer. Marsha Williams happened to be in the Fox office one day in 1992, and she saw the script for *Madame Doubtfire*. She read it but had reservations about the treatment of the story: "It was too broad and did not tell the story I felt it should tell."

Fox noted Marsha's interest and assumed that Robin was interested, too. They scouted around for a director and found Chris Columbus—who had had a very successful run with *Home Alone, Home Alone 2: Lost in New York.* Columbus said he would like to undertake the project with Williams.

There were meetings, and eventually Columbus rewrote the script more along the lines the Williamses suggested. Now, with a script acceptable to Robin Williams, Fox decided to do the picture.

Chris Columbus had turned the story into something that would appeal to adults as well as children—this was his particular talent, as the *Home Alone* series showed.

Briefly, the story line of the new script was as follows.

Daniel Hillard (played by Robin Williams) is an actor who does voice-overs for commercials and dramas but is a bit hard-nosed about what kind of voice-overs he will do.

When he is assigned a scene between a villainous cat and a victimized bird, in which the cat forces the bird to inhale a cigarette, Daniel insists on improvising antismoking dialogue so that kids will understand the horror of cigarettes. The company fires him.

Daniel then stays home to care for his three kids, since his wife, Miranda (played by Sally Fields), has a good job. One of the first things Daniel does is throw a big party for the children, but it gets out of hand and soon chaos reigns. Miranda stumbles into this, and there is a blowup.

They get a divorce, and Daniel is denied joint custody and granted only visitation rights, which are much too restrictive for him. This is a disaster for Daniel, who lives for his kids, but there is nothing he can do about it. He becomes depressed and can't even rouse himself to look for a job, until he sees a want ad for a nanny for three kids. Daniel knows who has inserted that notice—Miranda—and he knows just the man for the job.

Although the coincidence seems rather far-fetched, Daniel has a brother, Frank (played by Harvey Fierstein), who is a sensational makeup artist. Frank tries a couple of images for Daniel and finally gets the perfect one: "Mrs. Doubtfire."

As Mrs. Doubtfire, Daniel is disguised so well that Miranda does not recognize him. In fact, he is accepted by everyone as the new nanny, and he turns out to be the perfect nanny. Things settle down for a while until Miranda's old high school flame Stu (played by Pierce Brosnan) shows up.

At this point the action heats up a bit, but so do the laughs. The ending, however, created a crisis at the studio.

It mostly fell to Marsha Williams to fight for the "right" ending. What the studio brass and the publicists wanted was a snug happy ending, with Daniel and Miranda back together forever. The Williamses, on the other hand, wanted a bleaker ending, in which Daniel and Miranda never do get together again.

"Everybody," Marsha Williams said, "—our managers, our agents, people at the studio—said that the audience would want Daniel and Miranda to get back together, or, at least, to leave their situation up in the air." However, "when two people are harmful and wrong for each other, they do not belong together!"

As Robin put it: "The Norman Rockwell family doesn't exist. It's a myth."

The director elaborated, "Ninety percent of parents who separate don't get back together again. We don't want our audience to see a dishonest film. We didn't set out to make *The Parent Trap*. We're going to protect *Mrs. Doubtfire*. We're keeping it honest."

It looked as though there might be test screenings, with two endings shot and both shown to see which drew more praise.

However, Chris Columbus felt that "Test screenings don't matter. We just won't change it," he said. "Marsha and I are not going to bend." Thus in the end there were no test screenings. The brass finally caved in and did the ending the way the Williamses and the other actors wanted it.

The most crucial factor in the way Robin Williams would play the role of Mrs. Doubtfire was the disguise. This was a farcical situation, not a realistic drama. A woman, married to a man for fourteen years, was supposed not to recognize him as "Mrs. Doubtfire." Therefore, the disguise had to be right.

Robin Williams was appalled at some of the first attempts at this disguise. "Our early makeup tests, the ones with a lot of liver spots—it was like [in a stricken voice] 'What happened to her? Ohhh, she drank a lot!' Then finally they went to more of a glow, which is what a lot of these old Scottish women do have."

Another crucial element was Mrs. Doubtfire's voice. Marsha: "The voice was there from the very first makeup tests. We have a video of it—it was as if he had been instilled with the spirit of this woman."

But it wasn't really all that easy. Robin said: "We tried different voices—one that was [John Cleese doing Julia Child] much more, overly ripe, just frightening! The Dame Edna territory had already been staked out, and Dustin Hoffman staked out the southern accent, so you have to find something that's different."

Robin as Mrs. Doubtfire: "Oh yes, it's a greeeet thing to dooo on the phone if you don't want to talk to someone. Hellllooooo. . . . No, he's not here right now, dear. I'm very sorry about that. . . . Ohhh, that nasty salesman, really?"

The two men in charge of transforming Robin Williams into Mrs. Doubtfire were Greg Cannon and Ve Neill. "It took six weeks to design and create the appliances for the makeup," Cannon said.

Eventually, Mrs. Doubtfire's face consisted of eight overlapping foam latex appliances: one chin, two cheeks, a neck wraparound piece, one forehead piece, and two over-the-eye pieces. The eighth was a one-piece foam latex mask, which was used as a prop: Robin would peel it on and off as Daniel changed back and forth from himself to Mrs. Doubtfire.

"In the movie," Neill explained, "the character Daniel Hillard changes into Mrs. Doubtfire within a few moments. In actuality, the whole process, each time, took three to four hours to apply. We were on the shoot for forty days, so there was a lot of time in front of the mirror."

Lillian Ross covered the production for the *New Yorker*. "I was in the *Mrs. Doubtfire* production office on a Saturday afternoon when someone new walked in—a heavyset gray-haired woman wearing spectacles, a pleated plaid skirt, a white blouse with a Peter Pan collar pinned with a brooch, a wool cardigan sweater, stockings, and cornily sensible Oxfords. Graciously, and somewhat shyly, she wished me good afternoon in a charming, soft English accent." Lillian Ross didn't tumble—until later—to the fact that this was Robin.

Interviewing Robin for the *New York Times*, Maureen Dowd asked him: "So how does it feel to be, at last, a full-figured gal?"

Robin (in Mrs. Doubtfire's Scottish burr): "They're quite wonderful, these big, beanbag breasts are. It's great to be this blue-mouthed old lady, hitting on somebody, opening your blouse and saying, 'What about these?' "

Then, as a pitchman for Victoria's Secret, in a deeply sincere male voice: "Hi, I'm Robin Williams. You know, wearing these teddies is a choice I make. It's not just Glen-Blenda time for me. It's the nineties. It's a time for a man to feel comfortable all day. Teddies for men."

No one on the set was immune from Robin's riffs. He

loved to sneak up on Chris Columbus and snuggle against him. "Lay your head on my shoulder, you manly man. Oh, Christopher, you founded the country. Now take a moment for yourself, you hunk!" He would slink up on Marsha when she wasn't looking and cry out: "Honey, I love you! Give me a hug!" She would respond by staring at his bra straps and yelling: "This old lady is hitting on me!"

One day his costar, Sally Fields, walked right past him, not recognizing him through the makeup. And Robin's ten-year-old son came onto the set, took one look at his father, and went into a kind of slump.

Robin said. "My boy was like, 'Oh, great. Dad's dressing up like an old lady now. Hello, Geraldo.' "

Sometimes his antics simply took over the set. "Everybody sing!" he shouted at one juncture. He began humming the tune of "It's a Small World"—Disney's signature song. "It's a land of points you will never see," he sang. "It's all the profit going to me. We will keep all the bucks. You will go for the yucks. It's our world after all!"

They were filming in North Beach, California, and Williams loved to stop in at a newsstand in full regalia as Mrs. Doubtfire and look at the magazines. He was leafing through *Playboy* one afternoon, wearing his little blue gingham dress.

"That old lady is sure hip, man," remarked a startled college student surveying the scene.

"I feel so pretty!" Robin would cry out, tossing his head back and laughing. "As a larger, older woman, I feel very attractive, mainly to Teamsters and truckers. You know, men who aren't afraid of a woman who could both block and tackle if she got a job on the Forty-Niners.''

Chris Columbus spoke feelingly about working with Robin Williams: ''Yes, Rob is directable. I would say, 'Let's do it once the way I wrote it and then let Robin do whatever he wants.' ''

One of the key scenes in the movie—from the standpoint not of comedy but of pure emotion—is the confrontation when Miranda tells Daniel that she wants a divorce. Robin must convey shock, fear, and pathos in response to Miranda's anguish, frustration, sadness, and determination.

''I wanted the pacing to have the high and the lows when she tells Daniel 'It's over,' '' Chris Columbus said. ''And then I wanted it to take on a quiet. You film your peaks, and then you go into the editing room and find the perfect balance.''

And so it was with the confrontation scene. Columbus repeated the shot time and time again until Miranda spoke the words ''I want a divorce'' in the way he felt was right. He kept listening, and finally she said the words as simply and effectively as she could.

And as he heard the words, Robin Williams reacted to them with an expression of frozen agony.

''Cut!'' Columbus called out.

On the set, it was said, everybody was deeply affected. It was so quiet that you could hear breathing. Not a word was spoken. And then, with the scene done just the way he wanted it, Columbus let out a sigh.

Robin Williams was up on his feet, erupting into a riff. "You can have the upstairs!" he yelled in a Jewish accent. "I'll take the downstairs! You can't have the whole house! I'll bring witnesses!" And everybody started to laugh.

Columbus acknowledged that he had learned a lot from working with Robin Williams in this film, especially about female sensibility in men.

When *Mrs. Doubtfire* opened, there was carping from the critics, as usual, because of the farcical elements, but most of the negative comments were minor. In general, the critics found *Mrs. Doubtfire* far superior to Williams's previous picture, *Toys*, and it was acknowledged to be the kind of picture he could do better than many other actors. The following excerpts are typical.

Jay Boyar of the *Orlando Sentinel*: "Williams is so physically large in his Doubtfire drag that even the other characters comment on his size."

David Baron of the *New Orleans Times-Picayune*: "Chris Columbus's two-hour-plus farce takes way too long getting started (partly to accommodate a riff of less-than-fresh Williams imitations), but once Hillard has made himself over into Doubtfire, big laughs materialize. Williams as the grandmotherly governess is a scream."

Mrs. Doubtfire opened in late November 1993, during Thanksgiving week. The box office showed immediately that it was a hit, though how much of a hit could not be assessed right away. As the box-office numbers continued to improve, it was deemed a smash hit.

At first, before the picture began to gain real status—word of mouth gave it an added boost—some critics had complained that Robin Williams was doing nothing really new here; in contrast to Dustin Hoffman's performance as a woman in *Tootsie*. As the Christmas season passed, however, and the figures for *Mrs. Doubtfire* continued strong, the Hollywood Foreign Correspondents gave Robin the Golden Globe Award for Best Actor in a Comedy. This made the popularity of the film soar.

In the end, *Mrs. Doubtfire* grossed $219.2 million, more than any of Robin Williams's other films except *Aladdin*.

The consensus was that Robin Williams had succeeded in *Mrs. Doubtfire* and had proved that a failure like *Toys* did not mean he was washed up. It also opened the way for him to do something more daring than the roles he had been attempting.

Still, not everyone was happy with *Mrs. Doubtfire*. Dan Quayle, as vice president of the United States, had been championing what he called "family values," particularly in relation to marriage, divorce, and single parenting. Quayle was bothered by the ending, an epilogue that makes it clear that Daniel and Miranda are not about to walk off into the sunset together.

Robin pointed out that he and the filmmakers had intended to send a positive message—positive in the sense of being realistic rather than idealistic. "The reality in America—sad but true—is that divorce is up to about sixty percent, maybe higher, so second families move on from there," he said. "To have shown it otherwise would have been a negative fantasy. What I wanted to do was just try to put across something that my therapist was saying to me after my divorce. Just focus on your child. Try to make things better for him. That's the only thing I bring to it."

Chris Columbus agreed with Robin Williams about the ending. He had been instrumental in adapting the original script (by Randi Mayem and Leslie Dixon) to the realities of life in America. In fact, he had rewritten the ending with the full approval of Robin Williams.

Chris Columbus: "We wanted kids to know that their family, if they come from a divorced family, was just as valid as the family next door with two parents. Also, it was important that kids seeing this picture knew it wasn't their fault just because their parents got divorced. . . . We wanted a film which would be emotional where we could get a bit of a message across to kids."

The Perfect Plot

On May 27, 1995, the actor Christopher Reeve broke his neck during a riding competition. For at least five days his condition was precarious; his chance of surviving was at best fifty-fifty. Ultimately, Reeve was totally paralyzed by the accident.

In October of the same year he recalled: "I was hanging upside down [in a hospital bed], and I looked and saw a blue scrub hat and yellow gown and heard this Russian accent. There was Robin Williams being some insane Russian doctor."

Reeve burst out laughing. "I knew I was going to be all right," he said.

Robin's visit to the paralyzed actor was one of the bright lights of Reeve's early days dealing with his severe injury. Continuing his charade as a Russian visitor, Robin pretended to be a proctologist.

In October Reeve made a personal appearance in his wheelchair at New York City's Pierre Hotel, at the annual dinner of the Creative Coalition, an advocacy group for a number of issues including health care and funding for the arts. Reeve was copresident of the coalition, with actress Blair Brown.

Robin was present, too. He launched into ten minutes of jokes and riffs that included an offer to auction off Reeve's tie—which was actually his ventilator pipe. He concluded his standup with uncharacteristic earnestness— "You're on a roll, bro!"—but then he did the usual and gagged it up, adding, with a glance at the wheelchair, "Literally."

Robin's next motion picture assignment was to play Alan Parish in *Jumanji*, which was based on a board game and had all kinds of special effects and trick photography: it was an extravaganza of animatronic animals, computer graphics, floodwaters, mechanical puppets, and other eye-popping theatrical elements, like an extended thrill ride in an amusement park.

Robin found himself trying to explain what the word *Jumanji* meant, with the usual laughable results. "It means an Italian kosher restaurant," was one of his shots in the dark. "It's Hebrew al dente. God knows." Or maybe "It's an old word taken from Zulu, meaning 'many effects.' " Actually, it was the name of a town in a children's novel by Chris Van Allsburg.

In the board game Jumanji, the players take turns rolling dice and trying to advance along a track through a jungle in search of safety in a town called Jumanji. However, each square brings an attack by certain beasts of the jungle. In the story, the board game comes alive and the animals actually appear, thirsting for blood, in a house where the game is being played.

Van Allsburg's book is only twenty-eight pages long, and half of those pages are illustrations. As the screenplay expands on it, a boy, who is unhappy because his father derides him for not being macho, plays the game in 1969 with his girlfriend. On his second move he gets sucked into the board and vanishes from sight.

Twenty-five years pass. A brother and a sister move into the house, find the game, and start to play. This frees the earlier boy from the grip of the game; he is now an adult, played by Robin Williams.

The group continues to play the game, searching for Jumanji, the sacred town of safety and sanctuary. But terrible things happen to them. Animals of all varieties attack them. There are visual tricks galore: man-eating plants come to life; zebras, elephants, and rhinos appear. These terrors are enough to drive the characters crazy.

The animation underlines the dangers and seems to do the impossible—it makes the animals more vivid than those in real life. But because the animated animals were never visible to the actors on the set—the animals were drawn later and superimposed over the frames of film—the actors frequently had difficulty doing their scenes.

Robin explained, "The script called for me to look one way and say this or that with a certain expression, and they'd tell me things like, 'You're talking to the monkeys now.' They'd tell me the monkeys were very whimsical, so I could be whimsical. There'd be a monkey here, a monkey there. But then I might find out later that the monkeys were actually being completely hostile, and that I was looking at the wrong one while talking.

"It took concentration, total focus. Everywhere I'd turn these special effects guys would be putting down cue marks, and they tracked the shots with a huge, noisy high-tech camera that makes a grinding, whirring sound like a garbage disposal nipping at your face. It was a lot harder than interacting with real people. It was more like self-abuse with an oven mitt."

Jumanji also had a theme, of sorts. When Robin's character, Alan Parish, returns to the real world as a thirty-year-old, a strange boy-man, he discovers that his parents are dead, and this leaves many things in his life unresolved.

"Underneath is the real issue," Robin said. "If you had the chance to live over with your parents and make it right and make a connection with them, what a wonderful thing."

The reviews were mixed. Frank Gabrenya of the *Columbus Dispatch* wrote: *"Jumanji*—or *Honey I Stretched the Heck Out of the Book*—ought to be a holiday crowd-pleaser, although kids younger than eight or nine may find the movie's dangers much too real. Fans of the book, on the other hand, may wonder how they could have missed so many pages."

Paul Delean wrote in the *Montreal Gazette:* "Comic

actor Robin Williams has the key role of the adult Alan, but after a brash entrance looking like Robinson Crusoe, he's surprisingly restrained; it's as if he's deferring to the special effects.''

In 1978, a French-Italian film company made a comedy titled *La Cage aux Folles*, based on a French farce. It was an enormous hit, although most hard-nosed professional cineasts were puzzled by its popularity; it even made money in the United States, where moviegoers had to see it with subtitles.

La Cage aux Folles struck the fancy of Mike Nichols, the man responsible for several American film hits, including *Who's Afraid of Virginia Woolf?* (1966), *The Graduate* (1967), and *Carnal Knowledge* (1971).

"It's a perfect plot," Nichols said. "It's one of the great comedies of all time. It's an express train that comes bearing down on you. I've wanted to make the American version from the moment I saw the original."

It took sixteen years for him to secure the film rights. When he did, finally, in 1994, he began casting. Robin Williams was always at the head of the list, originally for the role of Albert, though he was eventually cast as Armand.

MGM-UA bought the rights. John Calley, UA's president, said, "I knew if Mike did it, we'd get top talent. I knew we'd get Robin Williams. So I said yes."

Top talent coalesced around Mike Nichols. Most important, he secured Elaine May, his former theatrical partner, to write the screenplay. She kept the surefire story line, which Nichols had called a "perfect plot," almost intact, but she Americanized the original details and updated what might be considered old hat.

The story involves two homosexual men, Armand (Robin Williams) and Albert (Nathan Lane). They are longtime companions who share an apartment on Miami's South Beach. Albert is the headliner at the Birdcage, a nightclub owned by Armand that features men in drag; he lives for his moments onstage as a drag queen. May changed the translation of the title (*The Cage of Fools*) to *The Birdcage* to indicate the importance of Albert's work at the nightclub.

Everything is normal at the Birdcage, and with Albert and Armand, until suddenly Armand's son, Val—the result of a heterosexual fling—announces that he is going to get married to the daughter of a right-wing politician (Gene Hackman). He wants his fiancée and her father and mother to meet his "parents." In a frenzy, the pair clean out their apartment, getting rid of its outrageous knick-knacks to prepare it for their staid guests.

Armand gives Albert lessons in appearing to be straight rather than flamboyantly homosexual, but Albert flunks the course again and again. Rather than let Albert attend the dinner party for their guests, Armand kicks him out.

Albert is incorrigible, however: if he can't be a host, he'll be a guest—and in the middle of the chitchat before the meal, he swishes in, done up in pearls, pumps, and a Barbara Bush wig, pretending to be Val's prim dowager mother.

The jokes escalate as the ridiculous farce goes on. In the end, as in all classic farces, order is more or less restored; the impossibilities are all sorted out, and possibilities have been substituted for them.

Robin Williams had no difficulty playing the role of a homosexual. "I grew up in San Francisco; I know many same-sex families," he said. "I tell people, 'They raise their children the same way you do—they love them. There are many kinds of family, not just the Norman Rockwell kind.' "

There was some improvisation. Even though Mike Nichols held the cast strictly to the written script, he did give Robin a certain latitude—what he called "permission to up the attitude."

In one scene, Robin improvised a line of dialogue that did not make it into the final cut. Val has just announced that he's marrying a girl. Robin improvised: "Where did we go wrong? Not enough opera and show tunes?"

Robin was amused at the cuts. "They should release a separate actors' cut," he said. But he defended Nichols's choices. "I have absolute faith that Mike knows what funny is. He was focusing on character and believability. At first I tried to kick it up a bit, and Mike said, 'No, just play your connection to your family and the love you have for Nathan, and then the comedy will play.' "

But one improvisation did make it into the picture. This was the scene in which Robin is trying to show Nathan Lane's partner on the stage of the Birdcage how to dance: the scene is a full-blown riff for Robin Williams.

"You do an eclectic celebration of the dance!" he cries out to Albert's clumsy partner (played by Luca Tommassini). "You do Fosse, Fosse, Fosse!" he chants, doing some classic hip-swiveling Bob Fosse moves. "You do Martha Graham, Martha Graham!" he says as he pulls his shirt over his head. Then he's Twyla Tharp, his entire body convulsed in trembling motion, segueing into a Michael Kidd Broadway jazz-prowl, and then careening on into Madonna and becoming a twisting, swirling tangle of naked arms above his head. Then, pausing for just a moment: "And you keep it all inside!"

Asked what inspired this, Robin explained: "It just came about. Armand is this choreographer. It came out in rehearsal one day."

When *The Birdcage* opened, the reviews were sharply divided: critics either loved it or hated it. This had also been true of the original French version; and, like the original, *The Birdcage* made more money than film people thought it would.

Much of the negative reaction could have come from homosexuals annoyed by the acting. Much of it could have come from people who had liked the French version and felt that the Americanized version had been corrupted by the rewriting.

Bruce Bawer wrote a harsh review for the *New York Times*. "They don't get gay life," he said later. "I saw the movie with a gay friend and we sat there in horror and disbelief, while the straight audience around us was just laughing it up."

"He says this isn't how gay people act?" Nichols responded. "Let him hang out with RuPaul for a couple of days. We're not just talking about gays—we're talking about drag divas, theatrical stars!"

Bob Fenster of the *Arizona Republic* hated the film: "As you may have noticed, almost anyone in Hollywood can make an unfunny comedy. But it takes major talents like Robin Williams and director Mike Nichols to make a dud as spectacularly clunky as *The Birdcage*."

But Owen Gleiberman reviewed it positively in *Entertainment Weekly*: "Written by Elaine May and directed by Mike Nichols, *The Birdcage* is an enchantingly witty and humane entertainment, a remake of the 1978 French farce *La Cage aux Folles* that actually improves upon its source."

The Birdcage was a strong contender at the box office from day one. The great word of mouth made it a must-see for filmgoers around the country.

There were several reasons for this success, and the most important was the acting ability and professionalism of Robin Williams. This is interesting, because at the beginning he had been of two minds about doing the picture—he had an aversion to doing a remake of what had become in French hands a classic motion picture. The first reason he finally caved in and said he would do it was the quality of the updated script, a brilliant remodeling of the French farce with just enough Americanisms and added wrinkles to provide something new for those who were familiar with the original. Second, he was getting a chance to work again with Mike Nichols—

the director who had inspired such fun and magic in *Waiting for Godot*.

A major factor in the success of this film was that Robin opted to play Armand rather than Albert. While people assumed that Robin was after a role he could play to the hilt, he fooled them all by deciding to do Armand, the less exhibitionist of the two gay lovers. This decision was not just instinctual; there was some interesting reasoning behind it. Robin had just done a very good job of appearing in drag as Mrs. Doubtfire, where he could work all kinds of magic around the role of a woman. Playing a flamboyant gay man, he felt, might draw comparisons between the two roles.

In leaving the wildly eccentric role of Albert to Nathan Lane, Robin effectively turned the relationship upside-down. Robin, the man everyone expected to be flamboyant and hammy, instead became the quiet, well-groomed, totally civilized half of the gay couple, leaving the acting tour de force to Lane.

The natural tension between the two actors became even more powerful, leading to scenes in which Robin was nothing more than a spectator at his partner's many send-ups and tirades. In effect, Robin Williams very simply handed the leading role to Nathan Lane and helped make Lane's excesses into something to relish and to laugh at.

The Birdcage grossed $124.1 million in the American market—scoring another breakthrough for Robin Williams.

Robin's next film, *Jack*, was about a boy trapped in the

body of a man. It was a fantasy, but it had more than fantasy going for it. Robin would be working with Francis Ford Coppola, who had directed the *Godfather I*, *II*, and *III* and *The Conversation*, along with other fantasies like *Peggy Sue Got Married* and thematic pictures like *Apocalypse Now*.

In fact, Robin had formed a partnership with Francis Ford Coppola and Robert De Niro, and the three of them had bought a restaurant in San Francisco. Robin said to one newspaper reporter: "I wanted to do *Jack* because of the chance to work with Francis. He had this three-week rehearsal period at his place in Napa, and I just sort of hung out with the kids."

Robin Williams also had other good reasons to play the part of Jack. "I could relate to Jack's desire to be with other children because I also lived in a big house on a lot of land, but way away from everybody else."

The juxtaposition of youth and old age in *Jack* fascinated Robin Williams. The protagonist is a child afflicted with a disease, largely fictitious but based on an actual ailment called progeria—premature old age. In the case of Jack, it is exaggerated to a monstrous degree.

At the age of one year, Jack Powell looks four. At five, he is an adult twenty. At ten, he's a forty-year-old man. It's a terrible fate. To prevent Jack from being hurt by the attention he might get from other children, his overprotective parents have kept him hidden away from prying eyes for ten years.

But now the tutor that his parents have hired—Dr. Woodruff (played by Bill Cosby)—advises them to put him in school and let him take his lumps. Although his parents are reluctant to subject him to stress and ridicule, they agree, and off to school he goes.

This is a typical Robin Williams role. He gets threatened by the other kids but manages to win them over when it turns out that he can play schoolyard games even better than they can, and he becomes a kind of hero. He has never before been with young girls or older women—except for his mother—and now he is putty in their hands. Much of the story centers on the schoolyard games, but Jack also joins the other kids in reading sex magazines in a hidden treehouse.

The reviews of *Jack* were uniformly bad, though most of them praised Robin's acting.

The year 1990 found Robin Williams in a time warp when he won the part of the first gravedigger in Kenneth Branagh's monumental uncut version of *Hamlet*. Robin was in a sense reliving his study of Shakespeare at Marin College.

Then he discovered that his old friend Billy Crystal had also won a role in *Hamlet*, so the two of them would be in England together. This was good news for Robin and Billy, but not necessarily for Kenneth Branagh.

Branagh did not usually run a tight ship, but once he had some indication of the endless horseplay that these irrepressible American comedians could indulge in, he sent down a command: Separate them. At no time should Robin Williams and Billy Crystal be on the set together—or so the story went.

Robin put the whole thing into focus later, in an interview in *People*: "I heard a rumor that Ken wouldn't allow me and Billy to be on the set at the same time. What did he think we would do? Riff? I can see it now: 'To be—or what?' "

Hamlet was the first time that Robin and Billy Crystal had worked together in a movie, even though their scenes did not overlap. As the first gravedigger—or first clown, as the role is described in the cast of characters—Robin hands the skull of Yorick to Hamlet. And, of course, Hamlet muses: "Alas, poor Yorick," and so on—one of the most memorable speeches in the play.

About Billy Crystal and himself Robin said, "We had always talked about working together, but it never happened." The fact that they were both billed in Branagh's *Hamlet* seemed enough to stir up interest in certain quarters of Hollywood.

In 1997, quite suddenly, Robin Williams and Billy Crystal were teamed together, in a film that looked like a potential box-office bonanza. It was called *Father's Day*, and it was scheduled to open near the actual Father's Day.

The success of *The Birdcage* had sent film moguls scurrying to look among foreign films for another farce—and they thought they had found it in a French picture that had opened in 1983: *Les Compères*. Like *The Birdcage*, this was a typical French farce, though it was a bit less lively and more sentimental than *The Birdcage*.

The title translates as "the pals," or "the buddies." It also has a slightly sly meaning—"con men," men engaged in a scam of some kind. In this case, though, the scam is worked on the two pals, not by them.

The buddies are Jack Lawrence (Billy Crystal) and Dale Putley (Robin Williams). As the story opens, a woman, played by Nastassja Kinski, calls on Jack, a hot-shot lawyer. She says that she's happily married but must tell him something. Seventeen years ago, Jack got her pregnant, though she never told him. A son was born, who has now left home and run off. She's desperate to get him back and feels that Jack—as his father—should be able to help. Jack agrees.

Then Kinski telephones Dale and gives him exactly the same story. Dale is an unhappy man—a born loser—on the verge of suicide, but the thought that he has a son energizes him. He feels he must help his old flame, and he gets right on the trail of the boy.

The two men bump into one another, since they are pursuing the same clues, and decide to work together, but neither admits to the other that he thinks he's the run-away's father. To the outside world, each man is undertaking the search strictly for Kinski.

Soon enough they find the boy, and he seems presentable to both of them. Each man, much to his secret joy, can see traces of himself in the kid. In the end, these two "pals" who actually have loathed one another from the start, become rejuvenated by the search and are better off for it.

Father's Day was heavily promoted by its stars, who are two of the most adept comedians in the business. Nevertheless, it did not do well when it opened, and the critics were turned off by it.

Good Hunting

There is one writer-director-actor in films whose latest project can always arouse interest. His name, of course, is Woody Allen.

In 1965, Allen wrote and acted in *What's New Pussycat?* The next year came *What's Up Tiger Lily?*, which he wrote, acted in, and directed. By 1969, with *Take the Money and Run*, Allen had become a sort of Renaissance man, producing a film a year on his own. Usually, the reception from fans as well as most critics was excellent. By 1997, Allen was a legend in the industry.

It was no surprise that Allen, who did all his casting by himself, face to face, became interested in whatever chemistry seemed to be working between Robin Williams and Billy Crystal in *Hamlet* and *Father's Day*. For his latest film, *Deconstructing Harry*, he hired both Williams and Crystal to join a large cast of stars including Allen himself, Kirstie Alley, Demi Moore, and Julia Louis-Dreyfus.

Crystal was the second lead in the film,

while Williams played Mel, a hapless fellow whose life is so unfocused that no one seems to notice him at all—in fact, every shot of Mel was deliberately out of focus. Mel had only a few scenes, and Robin took the job mainly in order to watch Woody Allen. But Robin Williams as Mel turned out to be the funniest gag in the movie, and he seemingly enjoyed every minute of it.

This picture became one of Allen's better attempts at his special brand of cinema. For Robin Williams and Billy Crystal, it was their third chance to work together. And there was another project in the works for Williams.

In the early 1960s, Disney had made a hit movie, *The Absent-Minded Professor*, starring Fred MacMurray. It became an icon as the highest-grossing movie of 1961, and led to a sequel called *Son of Flubber* in 1963. Now the Disney studios decided to redo the film and offered Robin Williams the MacMurray role.

The story concerns an invention dreamed up by the absentminded professor—"flubber," short for "flying rubber." The film was a wildly comic fantasy, with visual effects, photographed for laughs, piled one on top of the other.

People wondered why Robin had decided to do a strictly slapstick kid's film after his enormously successful appearance in *The Birdcage*. There was a very good reason. The story goes that Robin screened the original picture for his son Cody, then five years old, to see if his son liked it. When Cody loved it, Robin was convinced. He would do this picture "for the kids," as he put it. And so in *Flubber*

Robin Williams became the new absentminded professor, Phillip Brainard.

Because of the many visual effects, Robin found himself working again in exhausting aerial maneuvers. For example, at one point the flying rubber causes his car to levitate above the road, which meant that Williams had to don his aerial gear once more.

"I've got more flying time than Mary Martin," he noted, referring to her role as Peter Pan. Robin had used the same kind of rig in *Hook* and *Jumanji*. He explained it once:

"They have this thing called a nitrogen ram which pulls you up in the air. They can go fifty or sixty feet up if you want to go that high, and they can bring you down to within an inch of the floor—or through the floor if you choose—and then back up again fifteen or twenty times."

The hero of the film is flubber, not the absentminded professor. The invention of flubber saves ailing Medfield College, which is going broke. But Brainard doesn't realize how powerful the thing is. It begins to take over his life, much as the monster takes over Dr. Frankenstein's life.

The climax of the story is a college basketball game. The professor reduces the flubber to small quantities of liquid. He shows the basketball players how to rub the liquid flubber on their shoes—and when they walk or run, they look like a man on the moon going out for an evening jog and taking twenty-foot-long strides. The important game is won.

Flubber did very well at the box office the first weekend, but shortly thereafter the profits tailed off. The studio had been hoping for a $100 million gross, and the film didn't quite make that figure. Nevertheless, it was in the $90 millions, and very much alive.

Owen Gleiberman of *Time* wrote that the picture was "an agreeably unhinged slapstick jamboree." Indeed, "the special effects are the whole show, but there are far less entertaining things to see in a movie than Robin Williams being outacted by rocketing Jell-O."

As he had done so often in the past, for his next enterprise Robin Williams turned to almost exactly the opposite kind of motion picture, a perfectly straight story. The script had taken two young actors five years to write. Although both actors had had good roles previously, neither had caught fire. One of them was Matt Damon, an actor and playwright; the other was Ben Affleck, Damon's best friend. The two had known each other since they were in grammar school. They were both from South Boston, a rough-and-tumble part of the city, and they had the same dream about show business and Hollywood.

Matt Damon was a natural performer and athlete. When he graduated from Cambridge Rindge and Latin, a public high school, Damon entered Harvard as an English major, but he dropped out after three years to pursue an acting career. His interest in acting had been sparked by a one-liner role in the movie *Mystic Pizza*, a film that launched the career of the young Julia Roberts.

Ben Affleck had in the meantime moved to Hollywood with his younger brother, Casey Affleck, to make the rounds of the studios. The Affleck brothers were happy to put Damon up.

Ben Affleck got minor roles here and there and did well in Kevin Smith's *Chasing Amy*. Damon also did well once he got started. In 1996, he made *Courage Under Fire*, playing a heroin addict. He had starved himself to lose forty pounds for this role, and he had to eat his way back to health after the film was finished. Then Damon won the lead role in John Grisham's *The Rainmaker*, playing a naive lawyer who gets it into his head that he's going to do in an evil insurance company that is cheating its policy holders. But his ascension to superstardom came in Steven Spielberg's *Saving Private Ryan*, starring Tom Hanks.

For an English class at Harvard, Damon had written a one-act play about two kids who grew up in the toughest part of South Boston. Ben Affleck became interested in this play as soon as he found out about it. He and Damon decided to write a movie script based on it.

When Damon won the role in *The Rainmaker*, things began to heat up. The Miramax brass got quite interested in Affleck and Damon's notebooks and asked to see them. What they found there was a workable script.

In the script, Damon is Will Hunting, a janitor at Massachusetts Institute of Technology. Affleck plays a demolition worker, leaving all the weight of the story to Matt Damon.

The main plot turn is that Hunting, a troubled personality from his youngest years, gets into trouble with the law. But in spite of his serious personality disorders—the result of being abused as a child—Will Hunting is a mathematical genius. A professor (played by Stellan Skarsgaard) leaves a complex problem on the blackboard and after class watches Will Hunting solve it quickly and accurately. He then becomes interested in the personality and character of Will Hunting.

The professor eventually turns, in desperation, to an old pal who has done groundbreaking work with traumatized Vietnam veterans but is now embittered by the recent death of his wife. The friend, Sean McGuire (played by Robin Williams) brings Will Hunting out of his traumatic relapses to solve some of his problems.

Both Damon and Affleck told Miramax that they had a Robin Williams "type" in mind when they created Sean McGuire. When Robin saw the script and later met the young actors, he couldn't believe that so much intensity and reality could be generated by a couple of kids. "Let's see some I.D.," he told Damon with a smile. As he talked to the actors, he realized that these were dedicated professionals who knew what they were doing.

From that moment on, everything fell into place. Robin Williams was enthusiastic about the project. "This is something that I want to be a part of," he said. "It's a supporting part, but it's a great ensemble. It's just like being in *The Birdcage*. . . . I like being in a supporting part more than I like being a star. . . . For me it's just as meaningful and in some ways more relaxing to do that and to work with someone like Gus Van Sant" (Van Sant was the director of the film), "who's very relaxed."

After all, Robin went on, "I was training to be an actor. John Houseman said, 'Mr. Williams, you are damaged but interesting.' Part of what I hope to do eventually is to be acting once again."

One of the toughest scenes Williams ever played was between Will Hunting and Sean McGuire, when McGuire takes Hunting to Boston Common to talk.

The scene begins with the two of them sitting side by side on a bench, not looking at one another. For four minutes Sean talks about his wartime experiences in Vietnam and his life in Boston, and it is a telling scene because it reveals so much about Sean's early life.

A later scene connects with this, when everything breaks loose within Sean and the early, horrible years in South Boston flow out, revealing how he was savagely abused as a child.

Slowly, Will Hunting reveals that he, too, was abused. Sean assures him that it's not his fault. For the first time in his life, Will realizes that he has been carrying a burden but that he need not carry it any longer. This is a heart-rending and yet hopeful scene.

Good Will Hunting is a solid motion picture from start to finish. The theme of child abuse that runs throughout the picture is familiar, but this rather standard motivation does not prevent the viewer from becoming absorbed in the story.

It is Robin Williams's work that makes the whole movie worthwhile. In the very difficult passages between him and Damon, Williams pulls himself away from his natural actor's impulse to steal the scene; instead, he lets Matt Damon have his way and reacts only when he sees things getting out of hand.

Gus Van Sant has said that he did not really feel he had to do much to direct Robin Williams in his role. "I didn't have to do a lot of directing. I was possibly doing things intuitively."

When Robin first read the script, he warned Van Sant that he was going to do some things that he had never done before.

Van Sant: "I pretty much tried to stay out of his way and didn't give him specific pointers during the shoot. Generally, whatever I did say, he would disagree with." And so Van Sant kept his mouth shut. "My direction was more as an observer, making sure everything was going right and staying out of the way."

When Robin realized he was getting off track, he would ask for another run-through of the segment, usually making his interpretation sharper and more powerful the second time.

Ironically, Disney had been counting on *Flubber*, which did not do as well as expected; but *Good Will Hunting*, which was not expected to be a moneymaker, was doing well, in nineteenth position on the charts. It played on only seven screens, but it took in more than a quarter of a million dollars and played to sellout crowds where it did screen.

Hollywood began talking about the quick success of

the picture and the performance of Robin Williams. And, naturally, there were always murmurs about awards— maybe even Oscars. But 1997 was a tough year for supporting actors—Robin Williams's category. The competition was formidable: Robert De Niro was in the running for *Wag the Dog* and *Jackie Brown*. Anthony Hopkins and Morgan Freeman had supporting roles in *Armistad*. Burt Reynolds was up for *Boogie Nights*. Greg Kinnear was up for *As Good as It Gets*. Tom Wilkinson and Mark Haddy were up for *The Full Monty*. And Robin Williams and Ben Affleck were up for *Good Will Hunting*.

Burt Reynolds took the first round by winning the Golden Globe Award for his role as a porn-movie mogul in *Boogie Nights*. On the other hand, Robin Williams won Best Supporting Actor at the Screen Actors Guild (SAG) Awards. It was a tough night for Robin. "I was sitting over there sweating like Marlon Brando after Thai food!" he said. "I'm stunned," he went on, clutching the SAG award to his chest.

At the Academy Awards, Robin didn't know what to expect. He knew the odds were against him, and he had missed out when he did *Good Morning, Vietnam*. Nevertheless, it was already a good night for *Good Will Hunting*. The picture had received nine nominations, a very respectable number even for a hit movie. Also, Matt Damon and Ben Affleck were up for Best Original Screenplay.

In the end, Robin Williams won the Oscar for Best Supporting Actor. As he accepted the statuette, he embraced his good friend Billy Crystal, who was master of ceremonies that night.

Robin told Crystal: ''This might be the only time I'm speechless.'' But, luckily, he was not. He thanked his wife, Marsha, eloquently and then pointed to Matt Damon: ''Matt, I still want to see some I.D.'' Then he thanked his mother, and especially his father. ''I want to thank my father up there,'' he said, gesturing to the ceiling of the auditorium. Then he reverted to his usual form, became a hunched-over Groucho Marx in his duck walk, and padded off the stage with his Oscar gripped in his hand.

Later he said that he had really not expected this to happen. ''I didn't think I had a chance, and when they said it, I was shocked. This is a wild night. It's just insane. I'm very proud. This is an extraordinary piece and the first time I read it I wanted to do it.''

He had another thought to share. He had always known that the Oscars were prejudiced against actors who did comic roles, and he had always considered himself a comedian. ''Yes, I was trained as an actor. It's not like they had to medicate me. People think a comedian is a slightly damaged person. It's like, 'You're a comedian, go over there. Stay. Good.' ''

After *Good Will Hunting*, Robin turned his attention to a supernatural fantasy about the afterlife titled *What Dreams May Come*.

Robin Williams always loved to baffle anyone who

tried to predict what direction he was taking in his movie career, and *What Dreams May Come* offered another challenge.

The story involves a doctor named Chris Nielson, a typical family man, whose two children are killed in an automobile accident. Shortly after that, Chris himself is killed when he tries to help another accident victim. Chris's wife, Annie, played by Annabella Sciorra, is devastated and takes her own life.

Meanwhile, Chris finds himself in heaven, under the guidance and tutelage of a good angel, played by Cuba Gooding, Jr. Williams's character is determined to find his wife and to rescue her from her fate as a suicide. Gooding assures Chris that she's in a kind of hell because as a suicide she doesn't know she's dead.

The story follows Chris as he makes the journey to hell and back. He does find his wife, and there are long scenes between them. These scenes are tearjerkers. Though there are some lines of dialogue, there's also a great deal of weeping from Annie and moroseful looks from Chris.

Bob Fenster, a reviewer from the *Arizona Republic*, had this to say about the heavenly background, referring to the director, Vincent Ward: "Ward's visions of the afterlife provide the film's sole redemption." The movie, Fenster said, "is so incessantly treacly and morose that it's strictly for people who felt that there just weren't enough violins in *Titanic*."

Still, there are some good effects. Annabella Sciorra,

when she isn't sobbing, is a charismatic and charming wife for Robin Williams's doctor. And Cuba Gooding, Jr., takes the picture in hand and puts some magic into it. In his care, things look as they might in that heaven and that hell.

The story for Robin Williams's next film was based on a book by Patch Adams, *Gesundheit: Good Health Is a Laughing Matter*. In the film, Williams plays a young man named Hunter who, as a patient at a mental institution, gets the nickname "Patch" when he plugs up a hole in another patient's coffee cup.

In the 1970s, a physician named Hunter D. "Patch" Adams founded a hospital in the wilderness area of West Virginia, on 310 acres of land he bought on Droop Mountain. The hospital was not easily recognizable as such; it was at best a hodgepodge of buildings. It was called the Gesundheit Institute, and it was known locally as a reform movement.

It was a hospital without patients. There were only the two staff members who, like Patch Adams, believed in the healing power of humor and compassion.

But Patch Adams always insisted that with $25 million, a hospital would stand where the workshop and outbuildings stood, waiting to be incorporated into a much larger, true hospital establishment.

"It's like the end of most Frank Capra movies," Patch Adams said at his home in Arlington. He does not live at Gesundheit, but visits it regularly. "We're going to get the girl, get the business, and ride into the sunset."

Eventually, Adams enrolls at Virginia Medical College, where he breaks all the rules by circulating through the hospital at night, cheering up downcast patients. He is a believer in humor as the answer to every problem. As he drifts about, Adams gets the idea for Gesundheit, where he will care for patients with a smile and do everything he can to get them to feel good.

The picture of Robin Williams's face with a red bulb stuck to his nose is familiar to all movie fans—and quite probably to some people who are not fans—and one wonders if it is Patch Adams or Robin Williams who wants to save the world through laughter.

Patch Adams did not do badly at the box office. It opened on Christmas Day, 1998, and was solid from the start; by late January 1999, it had grossed $108.6 million, though the critics were unenthusiastic. When the *New Yorker* reviewed it, there was a warning at the end: "Good luck to Dr. Adams, but Dr. Williams should hang up his stethoscope, come down from Mt. Sinai, and get back in the pit with the real comics and the audience."

To many who saw it, the picture is a one-joke comedy, with Robin Williams in his red rubber nose playing for every laugh he can get.

The critics shook their heads, but it was obvious that whatever Robin Williams decided to do next, whatever his next character might be, his fans would be there with him—along with a lot of new admirers.

Whatever can be said about his selection of films, it is

obvious by now that Williams is one of those superstars who can promise big opening weekends and films with long runs. And with films like *Dead Poets Society* and *Good Will Hunting*, he's proved his ability to star in movies that draw Hollywood's highest accolades.

In early February 1999, *Patch Adams* had grossed $117.3 million and was still going strong. In its seventh week on the screens it had earned $122.5 million. Once again, Robin Williams had captured the hearts and laughs of audiences around the world.

Awards and Honors

1978   Emmy Award nomination, outstanding lead actor in a comedy series, for *Mork and Mindy*.

Golden Apple Award (also known as Discovery of the Year Award), Hollywood Women's Press Club, for *Mork and Mindy*.

1979   Golden Globe Award, best actor in a television comedy series, for *Mork and Mindy*.

Grammy Award, best comedy recording, for *Reality . . . What a Concept!*

Grammy Award nomination, best new artist.

1983   Grammy Award nomination, best comedy recording, for *Throbbing Python of Love*.

People's Choice Award, best male performer in a new television program, for *Mork and Mindy*.

1987   Academy Award nomination, best performance by an actor in a leading role, for *Good Morning, Vietnam*.

American Comedy Award, funniest male performer in a television special.

American Comedy Award, funniest male performer of the year.

American Comedy Award, best male standup comic.

Emmy Award, outstanding individual performance in a variety or musical program, for *A Carol Burnett Special: Carol, Carl, Whoopi*, and *Robin*.

Grammy Award, best comedy recording, for *A Night at the Met*.

1988　American Comedy Award, funniest male performer of the year, for *Good Morning, Vietnam*.

American Comedy Award, funniest actor in a motion picture, for *Good Morning, Vietnam*.

American Comedy Award, best male standup comic.

American Comedy Award, funniest male performer in a television special, for *Comic Relief II*.

Emmy Award, outstanding individual performance in a variety or music program, for *ABC Presents a Royal Gala*.

Golden Globe Award, best actor in a musical or comedy, for *Good Morning, Vietnam*.

Grammy Award, best comedy recording, for *Good Morning, Vietnam*.

Grammy Award, best children's recording, for *Pecos Bill*.

1989　Academy Award nomination, best performance by an actor in a leading role, for *Dead Poets Society*.

American Comedy Award, best male standup comic.

Golden Globe Award nomination, best actor, for *Dead Poets Society*.

Hasty Pudding Man of the Year, Hasty Pudding Theatricals, Harvard University.

1990 American Comedy Award, funniest male performer in a television special, for *Comic Relief III*.

1992 Academy Award nomination, best performance by an actor in a leading role, for *The Fisher King*.

Golden Globe Award, best actor in a musical or comedy, for *The Fisher King*.

Golden Globe Award, special achievement, for *Aladdin*.

ACE Award, National Cable Television Association, for *Comic Relief*.

1993 Golden Globe Award, best actor in a comedy, for *Mrs. Doubtfire*.

1998 Academy Award, best supporting actor, for *Good Will Hunting*.

Screen Actors Guild Award, best supporting actor, for *Good Will Hunting*.

1977–1978   *Laugh-In*, NBC.

1978   *Battle of the Network Stars*, ABC.

1982   Host, *E.T. and Friends—Magical Movie Visitors* (documentary), CBS.

I Love Liberty, ABC.

1983   *An Evening with Robin Williams*, HBO.

1985   *Richard Lewis I'm in Pain Concert*, Showtime.

1986   Host, *Comic Relief*, HBO.

Comic Relief: Backstage Pass (documentary), HBO.

Barbra Streisand: One Voice, HBO.

Robin Williams: An Evening at the Met, HBO.

The Young Comedians All-Star Reunion, HBO.

Cohost, *Fifty-eighth Annual Academy Awards Presentation*, ABC.

1987   *A Carol Burnett Special: Carol, Carl, Whoopi, and Robin*, ABC.

Host, *Will Rogers: Look Back in Laughter* (also known as *Will Rogers: An American Hero*), HBO.

Superstars and Their Moms, ABC.

Comic Relief II, HBO.

Tommy Wilhelm, "Seize the Day," *Great Performances*, PBS.

Jonathan Winters: On the Ledge, Showtime.

1988 *Jonathan Winters Special*, Showtime.

ABC Presents a Royal Gala, ABC.

An All-Star Celebration: The '88 Vote, ABC.

"An All-Star Toast to the Improv" (also known as "An All-Star Salute to the Improv"), *HBO Comedy Hour*, HBO.

Sixtieth Annual Academy Awards Presentation, ABC.

The Comedy Store Fifteenth Year Class Reunion (also known as *Comedy Store Reunion*), NBC.

Free to Be . . . a Family, ABC.

1989 Host, *Comic Relief III*, HBO.

The Barbara Walters Special, ABC.

The Prince's Trust Gala, TBS.

Saturday Night Live Fifteenth Anniversary, NBC.

1990 Host, *Comic Relief IV*, HBO.

An Evening with Bette, Cher, Goldie, Meryl, Olivia, Lily, and Robin, ABC.

Time Warner Presents the Earth Day Special, ABC.

"The Walt Disney Company Presents the American Teacher Awards," *The Magical World of Disney*, The Disney Channel.

1991 *The Dream Is Alive: The Twentieth Anniversary Celebration of Walt Disney World*, CBS.

Entertainers '91: The Top Twenty of the Year, ABC.

Talking with David Frost, PBS.

1992 *Dame Edna's Hollywood*, NBC.

Host, *Comic Relief V*, HBO.

The Whoopi Goldberg Show, as a guest, syndicated.

Comic Relief V, HBO.

The Tonight Show with Jay Leno, NBC.

1993 *The Late Show with David Letterman*, CBS.

1994 *Homicide*, guest appearance, NBC.

Comic Relief VI, HBO.

In Search of Dr. Seuss, TNT.

1995 *Dolphins*, documentary star and host, PBS.

Comic Relief VII, HBO.

1996 *E! Entertainment Television*, interviews and appearances, E!

1980   Title role, *Popeye*; Robert Altman, director; Paramount.

1982   T. S. Garp, *The World According to Garp*; George Roy Hill, director; Warner Bros.

1983   Donald Quinelle, *The Survivors*; Michael Ritchie, director; Columbia.

1984   Vladimir Ivanoff, *Moscow on the Hudson*; Paul Mazursky, director; Columbia.

1986   Jack Dundee, *The Best of Times*; Robert Spottiswoode, director; Universal.

Jack Moniker, *Club Paradise*; Harold Ramis, director; Warner Bros.

1987   Adrian Cronauer, *Good Morning, Vietnam*; Barry Levinson, director; Buena Vista.

Narrator, *Dear America* (also known as *Dear America: Letters Home from Vietnam*); Bill Couturie, director; Taurus Entertainment Company.

1989   King of the Moon, *The Adventures of Baron Munchausen*; Terry Gilliam, director; Columbia/TriStar.

John Keating, *Dead Poets Society*; Peter Weir, director; Buena Vista.

1990   Joey O'Brien, *Cadillac Man*; Roger Donaldson, director; Orion.

Dr. Malcolm Sayer, *Awakenings*; Penny Marshall, director; Columbia.

1991   Dr. Cozy Carlisle, *Dead Again*; Kenneth Branagh, director; Paramount.

Parry, *The Fisher King*; Terry Gilliam, director; TriStar.

Peter Banning/Peter Pan, *Hook*; Steven Spielberg, director; TriStar.

1992   Voice of Batty Koda, *Ferngully: The Last Rainforest* (animated); Bill Kroyer, director; Twentieth Century–Fox.

Leslie Zevo, *Toys*; Barry Levinson, director; Unknown.

Voice of the Genie, *Aladdin* (animated); John Musker and Ron Clements, directors; Disney.

1993   Title role, *Mrs. Doubtfire*/Daniel Hillard; Chris Columbus, director; Twentieth Century–Fox.

Hector, *Being Human*; Bill Forsyth, director; Warner Bros.

1995   Alan Parish, *Jumanji*; Joe Johnston, director; TriStar.

1995   John Jacob Jingleheimer Schmitt, *To Wong Foo, Thanks for Everything, Julie Newmar*; Beeban Kidron, director; UK.

1996   Armand, *The Birdcage*; Mike Nichols, director; MGM-UA.

Title role, *Jack*; Francis Ford Coppola, director; Buena Vista.

The Professor, *The Secret Agent*; Christopher Hampton, director; UK.

First gravedigger, *Hamlet*; Kenneth Branagh, director; UK.

1997   Dale Putley, *Father's Day*; Ivan Reitman, director; Warner Bros.

Professor Phillip Brainard, *Flubber*; Les Mayfield, director; Disney.

Sean McGuire, *Good Will Hunting*; Gus Van Sant, director; Miramax.

1998   Chris Nielson, *What Dreams May Come*; Vincent Ward, director; UK.

Title role, *Patch Adams*; Tom Shadyac, director; UK.